This is Jenny To Kristan's
Special copy of

What Rhymes with Bastard?

Signed on 7·11·08 at 6·15pm
by the author while
recovering from an icecream.

Linda Robertson XOX

LINDA ROBERTSON

What Rhymes with Bastard?

FOURTH ESTATE · *London*

For my mother

First published in Great Britain in 2008 by
Fourth Estate
An imprint of HarperCollins*Publishers*
77–85 Fulham Palace Road, London W6 8JB
www.4thestate.co.uk

Visit our authors' blog: www.fifthestate.co.uk

1

A catalogue record for this book is available from the British Library

ISBN-13 978-0-00-723225-3

Typeset in PostScript Minion by
Rowland Phototypesetting Ltd, Bury St Edmunds, Suffolk

Printed in Great Britain by Clays Ltd, St Ives plc

CONTENTS

Hmm, let's see . . .

Astard
Castard
Dastard
Eastard . . . no.
Fastard
Gastard
Hastard
I . . . no.
Jastard
Kastard
Lastard
Mastard . . . mastered? No.
Nastard
O . . . no.
Pastard – plastered? Plastered!

This is the story of how a very nice boyfriend became a Plastered Bastard and how I wrote some songs about it.

Part One: *The End*

1: Me, Jack, and Me and Jack

*'Don't try and change anyone, Linda. I thought I
could change your father. You can't do it.'*

Mum

Before everything turned to shit, Jack was my most successful project
ever. He was nineteen when I met him, and as much of a mess as
his bedroom. Instead of buying food, he spent his student grant on
speed, acid, ecstasy and marijuana, surviving on nibbles 'borrowed'
from the communal fridge. He always left a regretful note, gracious
but with no mention of imminent replacement:

Dear John,
I'm so sorry. I took your cheese.
Jack.

I started to collect them. I noticed he chain-smoked roll-ups,
went to bed at nine a.m., and drew self-portraits in charcoal on his
bedroom walls, incurring the wrath of the college authorities. A
little crowd would gather in his room to witness his battles with
the head cleaning lady: Brenda, screeching, hands on hips, Jack
with his eyes still shut, making polite sounds from his bed. I found
this endearing, but some of his strange practices were definitely
negatives:

- A tendency to recite Nietzsche in inappropriate social settings
- A disinclination to wash
- Going barefoot (which was OK in itself but incurred ridicule from my friends)
- Walking with a chimpanzee-like stoop
- Holding his feet at right-angles
- Getting stoned to slow down and taking speed to speed up again
- Refusing to exercise or even walk on an incline

I considered this list, then I considered the positives: he was tall, handsome, gentle and sweet, and his ineptitude was charming. I knew a good fixer-upper when I saw one. With the maturity of a twenty-two-year-old I set about the repairs.

Five years later I had a fully functioning boyfriend, ensconced within a highly functional relationship, in which life tasks were assigned according to skill sets. Jack handled the higher issues, deciding which books and films were admirable, who was smart, what was right and – most importantly – what was wrong. I took care of the day-to-day stuff, selecting our clothes, furniture, housing, careers, friends and social activities. Household bills, naturally, were always in my name.

Thus far, my project had failed on only two fronts. The first of these was the inordinate amount of time Jack spent on writing projects. During a week-long holiday in 1998, he whiled away thirty-five documented hours writing a two-page letter to his best friend's mum. Most of his spare time had been poured into a foot-high stack of works-in-progress. I had, admittedly, made some headway by turning him into a copywriter. Churning out text by the yard had increased his pace, but it was still a source of contention. My other failure was Jack's smoking. He'd been at it for fifteen years and already had circulation problems – a large varicose vein had appeared in his crotch, coiling across his scrotum and up his cock like a power cable.

Achieving this tightly regulated relationship hadn't been easy. About three months into our courtship, he went temporarily insane and had to be locked up. It was the Easter holidays, and I was stuck at Mum and Dad's house, waiting for my new boyfriend to arrive from London. By the time he was eight hours late, I gave up, dried my tears and went off to visit a friend in Southampton. Mum phoned us later that afternoon.

'Hello, darling,' she said. 'I've just had a call from a girl who said she was ringing from a mental hospital in Woking. She said she was a fellow patient of your friend Jack's. What should I do?'

The next day, I drove the hundred miles to the hospital, where I found my new boyfriend hopping round a traffic cone. 'Hi, Bunny!' Still hopping, he jiggled my shoulders. I asked him what had happened.

'The pigs got me!'

'How did they get you, Jack?'

'Ha ha! They said, "You can do this the easy way or the hard way," and I said, "The hard way!" So they beat me up, but it took three of them! Look!' He showed me a nasty crop of bruises.

Later I pieced together the events: after taking the usual cocktail of speed, acid, dope and ecstasy, he had gone to London and begun a mystical quest for his dad, whom he had never met. He decided his philosophy professor was the most likely candidate, and wrote him a series of impassioned letters, hanging some on trees and posting others, which were later returned in a sealed envelope. He walked around naked in High Barnet, reciting from *Ecce Homo*, which promptly got him arrested and banned from the borough.[1] That was where his friend lived, so now he had nowhere to stay. He

1 High Barnet police are notorious for their poor taste in literature.

decided to build a raft and escape down the Thames, so he dumped his belongings in the tube station and made his way to Camden Lock, where he started throwing planks and branches into the canal, which wasn't a river but would do at a pinch. He needed to steer his vessel and spotted an ideal-looking mop on top of a narrow-boat. He ran on board to fetch it, but the owner got upset and called the police.

Jack resisted arrest with the mop and was taken to the cells, where the police psychiatrist decided he was mad, and ordered him put away somewhere else. As all the local NHS wards were full, he was sent to a private hospital on the outskirts of Woking – Willowdell Hall – which took a very relaxed stance towards recovery, as the owners got £300 per patient per day from BUPA or the NHS. In return, they hung crap oil paintings on the walls, and made fancy food. ('Good evening, Mr Stumford, will you have banoffee pie or peach melba tomorrow night?') This last luxury was a bit of a waste, as most of the patients were anorexic.

On my second visit to Willowdell Hall, I met Jack's mother. She was surprised by my loyalty – as her son didn't seem like good boyfriend material, even to her. She told me how she had raised Jack on her own after having been abandoned by a rich American who had got her pregnant. After the drama of the birth, she'd fallen unconscious and then woke up in a hospital in America quite alone. Where was her baby? Dragging her drip behind her, she'd found him spreadeagled beneath a knife, moments away from circumcision. 'Get your hands off my beautiful boy!' she'd snarled, and snatched him back, then limped off to bed; next, she'd taken him back to Wales, where they'd lived with her sister's family while she retrained as a nurse, working nights, studying by day and forswearing sleep and sex. It was there that Jack grew to manhood with his foreskin intact, surrounded by women, hens and puddles. And it was there, as the damp months turned slowly to years, that he grew a pair of size thirteen feet.

Back in Woking, the doctors had no idea when – or even if – he'd recover. I visited him every day, hoping things would get better, but they didn't. Private clinics don't accept dangerous patients, so he was the only male resident. A three-strong harem formed round him, solemnly following him through the grounds, giving him shoulder massages. By flirting with one, he provoked me into having sex with him. His bed collapsed. He had to get a new one, and it was obvious why.

Willowdell Hall was not locked, and Jack went missing on a daily basis. He was often found standing on the road out front, directing traffic with volumes of nineteenth-century poetry.

After three weeks of this sort of thing, I had to return to Cambridge to face my final exams – three years of indolence distilled into six weeks of hell. When Jack and I argued on the phone one night, he tried to escape to Cambridge by hitch-hiking up the M1, and was quickly picked up by the police. I decided I needed to visit him again, but the day I arrived, he suffered a bad reaction to his medication, and things got really nasty. He started saying creepy things, and dribbling, and then his face froze, whereupon the nurses dragged him upstairs, pulled down his jeans and gave him a massive injection in the backside. At once he fell asleep, and I went home.

All too soon, my exams began. While I tackled Paper 7: Near-identical Portraits of Fat Old Men in Wigs, 1740–1860, my mum took my boyfriend out for afternoon tea, accidentally driving the wrong way up a motorway slip-road. 'Christ, Lins, your mum's insane!' he yelled, into the phone.

'Oh, darling,' reported Mum, gaily, 'Jack's a riot! We were in this café run by Christians and he went up to the owner and said, "You know, I don't believe in God," and then had this philosophical conversation with him and, of course, the owner couldn't keep up. Oh, it was marvellous!' I was glad they were having fun.

While I struggled with Paper 8: Near-identical Classical-style

15

Buildings in Varying States of Disrepair, 1000 BC – the Present, my parents took Jack out to the Woking shopping centre. 'And, darling – he disappeared! We thought he'd escaped. He was gone for at least half an hour, and we were panicking. We were thinking we'd have to call the police – oh, it was terrible, I had such a fright, because we were legally responsible for him! And then he came out of the gents', smiling as if nothing had happened.'

'Mum, I should have warned you – Jack takes for ever in the loo.'[2]

Things took a turn for the worse. A bed had come up in an NHS place in Cambridge, and he was being transferred. He was happy that he'd be closer to me, and so was I, until I visited him. It was like one of those re-enactments of nineteenth-century Bedlam you see on BBC2, and the place stank of ladies' pants. Not surprisingly, he got better pretty fast. That summer, his mum got him a job moving furniture, and watched over him while he got his head back in order. Altogether, it had been a humiliating episode. Jack had no more secrets. Those who cared for him had been hurt, and everyone else was laughing. He loved drugs, but it was official: he couldn't handle them, and it was my responsibility to make sure he never took them again.

These were the inauspicious beginnings of our story. Not the ideal basis for a solid relationship, you might think, but the fact is, I'd never had a boyfriend before. My mother was beginning to despair, so even a boyfriend in a lunatic asylum seemed better than none. I felt the same way.

2 I have calculated that, over the years, I have spent around 250 hours waiting for Jack in similar circumstances.

I was a teenage solipsist

My early childhood was spent almost exclusively with my mum, a devoted and endlessly interested companion. Her friends' kids were older than I was, and Dad was busy with his crossword, so it was just the two of us. Perhaps as a result of this, I pursued close one-on-one friendships with a single-minded passion from the moment I was pushed into the social whirl of nursery school. When I made a friend, I didn't want to share her, and I was never the first to let go. I spent most of my childhood lying in bed, reading – a delicious habit that has the preservative effects of heroin but doesn't build one's social skills.

Significant Best Friend No. 1 was Melanie. Aged eleven, we dressed up as pigs and became fast friends. We'd go to jumble sales, then totter home in the worst possible outfits, giggling helplessly. As I was copying her, I'd got Mum to buy me a coat just like hers, from C&A, and we used to hold hands within the matching sleeves. But one year later we were marched off to different schools: I was sent to the local comprehensive, five years of breeze-block hell. Melanie started seeing boys and forgot about me. Aged sixteen, I got a job on the till in the Safeway opposite her house and sat on the fire escape, staring at her and her spotty beau as they walked to the bus stop. I went to her birthday party in my brown Safeway uniform, accessorized with tan tights. As I sat in silence, a blond boy approached. 'Excuse me,' he said, 'but do you have any friends?'

I worked at Safeway for £1.79 an hour three nights a week. At all other times, I watched TV. On Saturdays, I played the violin in a youth orchestra until one p.m., then went home and went to bed for the rest of the weekend. For recreation, I ate microwaved muffins and jam, and watched TV. Sometimes I just lay there, looking at my bedroom wall, willing time to pass, waiting to become an adult. Nobody intervened: they don't really fuss about teenagers who do well at school.

I found someone who hated everyone else as much as I did, and we both dressed up as Christmas trees for non-uniform day in June – an anti-fashion protest that aroused great hostility. That was fun, but it was with unmitigated joy that I left the breeze-block gulag behind. Mum bought me a bus pass and I trekked to Winchester for my A levels. I had a bottle of whisky in my bag, and I'd started reading again, but I was still listening to Bartók and acting aloof. One day, a girl at school made a comment about the rain, and I told her I didn't have a faculty for discussing weather.

Luckily, Significant Best Friend No. 2 saved me from social death. Alice was the world's cutest Catholic. She had the button nose, the boobs and the confidence to attract a steady line-up of boys. Her friendship helped me eke out a paltry social life, which pleased my mum. While others my age had curfews and the like, she would happily come and pick me up at all hours from a club, a house, a bar or – more likely – the forty-seven bus stop, where Alice and I spent much of our time.

One person is one thing, but several people are quite another. If the evening involved more than the two of us, I'd spend it on a knife edge, striving so hard to impress people that I'd forget to be nice. To be honest, it never occurred to me to be nice in the first place. I'd never liked groups of people. In junior school I'd giggle away in lessons, then squirm with anxiety as break-time approached. I'd march up and down the playground on my own, practising my whistling. In secondary school, I clung to the periphery of groups, and when it got too much, headed for the library cupboard or the toilet.

I was usually second to last to be picked for teams, one up from the fat kid, and always found myself at the end of the row. I would clam up, then hate myself for it. Not that anyone would have noticed: they were all too busy worrying about themselves. That's the trouble with solipsism – you think you're the only one.

By the time I could finally drink and drive legally, I sensed Life just beyond my grasp. I was certain it would begin for real once I got to university. I'd find a little gang of people who were just like me. (Of course, had I actually met anybody just like me, I wouldn't have liked them.) I couldn't wait, so I didn't, despite the social pressure to take a year off and 'see the world'. I had other reasons to avoid the world, too, and as this stay-at-home stance helped shape my future, I'll explain a few.

1. I couldn't imagine enjoying myself, no matter where I went.
2. Financing the expedition would have necessitated six to nine months' hard labour behind a till or a bar, earning £2 an hour. I could have done it with student loans, but in a household where only the house was bought on credit, such lavish expenditure was unthinkable, and under Mum's eagle-eyed surveillance, I couldn't pretend I'd gone to the Isle of Wight instead of Cameroon.
3. I had no one to go with, as Alice was in Poland, and travelling alone is only fun if you like talking to and/or sleeping with strangers. I envisaged myself alone in Thailand, relaxing with date-rape drugs and falling off elephants, fending off Brazilian street kids, swimming in corpse-laden Indian rivers, staggering forlornly up the Himalayas, contracting malaria, playing host to tropical parasites, or (more likely) watching French TV alone as an au-pair.

In October 1991, I arrived at university in a delightful floral dress. No one was impressed.

'Why do you dress like that?' said one.

'Hmm,' said another.

'You like to be noticed, don't you?'

Look closely at our freshers' photo, and you'll see tears in my eyes.

On the first night of term, there was a power-cut, and I retreated to my room. I was alone in the dark with a daddy-long-legs. I tracked my new friend as he buzzed across the ceiling in the yellow glow from my bike light, casting a gigantic, sinister shadow. Across the gardens, a crowd in the college bar enjoyed the thrill of the black-out. I fell asleep to the muffled sound of squeals and laughter.

I'd arrived at college unkissed, as insecure as I was arrogant. Hard to approach, and less than beautiful, I continued not to be kissed. The longer this went on, the harder it got to kiss me. When a bitchy boy told me I was predatory, I stopped wearing dresses and switched to pyjama trousers with baggy sweaters. I longed for a lover to halt the vicious cycle. Had I known that one day he'd just walk into my room, I could have saved myself a lot of hassle. While other girls seemed to get drunk, then wake up with a new boyfriend, nothing happened to me, no matter what I did.

I unwittingly got myself cast as a dominatrix in a play about masturbation: nothing (although, years later, the director sent me love packages, one of which contained a photo of my corseted self wielding a whip). I joined Footlights and played the part of a tree: nothing. I sent a red paper heart to a Catholic rugby player, who liked guilty one-night stands with short, busty girls: nothing. I told A to tell B that I liked B without realizing that A was in love with B: nothing. I spent the night in London with a curly-haired idiot film-maker, who got me into his bed, asked how many men I'd 'had', then leaped to the far side of the bed when I told him. I went on a blind date with Ali G.

Of course, Ali G didn't exist back in 1992, so I was actually out on the town with plain old Sacha Baron Cohen, a second-year history student, currently playing the lead in *Fiddler on the Roof* at the Amateur Dramatics Club. Hundreds of us were out on random dates that night, as part of a fund-raiser, but Sacha had got to choose his date because his friend was organizing the whole thing. He claimed I'd written the funniest application form, but I suspect he'd been swayed by my self-description as 'blonde, busty and six feet tall'. He did seem a bit disappointed.

'You're not blonde.'

'No.'

He was confident, charismatic, funny, and corrected my English very nicely. He was also, not surprisingly, incredibly popular. We stood outside the local kebab shop in a sea of his friends, and from time to time, he'd put his arm round me and say, 'This is my blind date!' A little cheer would go up, after which I'd return to my chip butty. Still, I must have done something right, because I got to hang out with him and his friends a few more times. I adored Sacha, and Sacha's friend adored me. The friend was sporty and a bit bland, with the same private-school glow of confidence. Aside from the full-length Barbour coat, he was perfectly acceptable – a nice posh football-player. We went to a party together where I drank red wine, which made me want to throw up. 'There's a spare room at my place,' said the friend, 'and I live just round the corner.' In fact, he lived about a mile away, and the spare room, I realized gradually, was his bedroom. Even though I kept saying, 'I want to puke,' he started dancing with me, then lay on the bed with me and kissed me. Or tried to. I broke away from his embrace, and eventually he fell asleep. At dawn, I sneaked away.

Looking back, it strikes me that he would have been a good one to start with, but I had aspirations beyond sportswear – a cricket jumper here, a baseball cap there – and was looking for an artist or a philosopher. Or maybe a piano-player.

By the end of my first year, I was the only virgin left, outside the computer science department. EVERYONE else had done it, at least once. Everyone. My last romantic relationship had been in 1979, with an eight-year-old boy who lived next door to my nan.

Given the intensity of my same-sex friendships, my mum would occasionally make enquiries about lesbian activities: 'But what do they *do*, Linda? Do they use a carrot?'

21

To help me cope, I told myself that I could never have a boyfriend because there was something wrong with me, and that was absolutely fine because if I didn't find one by the time I was twenty-five I would kill myself, and then I couldn't be alone for ever, just three more years, max.

October 1994. I was about to start my final year at university and I was still a goddamned virgin. Sighing, I booked myself into a house full of strangers because there was a gigantic room available, and, as it turned out, four of them were cute: four under one roof! There was the tall guy with the stoop – I liked him because he'd been to art college and didn't wear shoes, and all my friends thought he was a ridiculous, pretentious twat. Then there was the really good-looking tall one with the bowl cut, and the massive tall one with the Yorkshire accent, and the sweet scientist in the room opposite. I couldn't cope with all the pressure so I hid in my room and took to peeing in a cup.

Jack – the tall one with the stoop – was intrigued by my air of mystery. One day, he took a phone message for me and then a rare proactive step: he crossed my threshold. I was thrilled – he was in my room! I put the kettle on to boil, and so began his primitive courtship ritual:

1. coming down the stairs and entering my room;
2. sitting in a chair reading a book;
3. not leaving unless explicitly told to.[3]

He wasn't much of a talker. One night I gave up hope of conversation and – kind of wishing he'd leave and kind of wishing he wouldn't – fell into an exasperated, self-conscious sleep while he sat in my chair, quietly reading *The English Auden*. When I woke up

3 Stages 2 and 3 were facilitated by constant marijuana use, which left no money for food – hence the kitchen 'borrowing'.

the next morning, the scene was exactly as I'd left it, except he was three-quarters of the way through the great red tome. A few nights later, he sat in the same chair and began to read *Heart of Darkness* aloud. I was half bored, half charmed and half asleep to boot. Throughout the night I drifted in and out of consciousness (in retrospect a great way to soak up this delirious tale). Once he'd finished reading, he asked if he could curl up on my bed. I nodded. This went on for several nights, until eventually he plucked up courage to ask to sleep next to me. The weight of his arm round me kept me as wide awake as if it had been a cattle prod. A quiet, trembling joy was bubbling up within me and it was all I could do to keep the lid on. Afterwards when my lumbering suitor was around, I came over all jittery and busied myself with constructing elaborate toasted sandwiches.

He couldn't work out what was going on. 'Excuse me,' he asked, 'but do you have a boyfriend?'

Adrenalin rushed through me – was I going to *be sick*? Here was the gigantic, earth-smashing moment I'd been waiting for: at last, something was going to happen! 'Um, no,' I replied, looking intently at my knee.

'Right.' He nodded.

Sharing a fondness for playgrounds, we'd go on moonlit walks in search of swings. Our favourite park not only had an on-site chip shop but a slide with a wooden Wendy house at the top. We'd climb up and shelter from the rain, chips steaming in our laps. He'd give me 'blowbacks' from his joints, bringing his lips perilously close to mine and stunning me into silence for moments at a time. I wasn't into drugs, except on prescription, but it seemed the friendly thing to do. Maybe I'd learn to like them.

Finally he asked if he could kiss me.

Here was the man I would love for ever. And yet I was furious if he was still there when I woke up in daylight because I didn't like being looked at. I thought he would notice my face and realize he'd made a mistake. But the days went by and he continued to reappear. He often came to my bed after using drugs, going to sleep at dawn and refusing to budge until well into the afternoon. The college cleaner would come in at eleven a.m and roll Jack on to the floor where he'd lie, snoring, then crawl back between clean sheets. I did my best to keep our relationship a secret, but in such circumstances it wasn't possible.

That was about all we did for the first three weeks until, during a heavy-petting session, he asked politely to move things forward. I consented – I'd already gone on the pill. Physically, the experience was no more stimulating than my annual date with a speculum, and certainly didn't match up to the relief and pure joy of being able to say without blushing, at long, long last, that I was a Virgo. For the entire minute and a half, all I was thinking was 'OH, MY GOD! I'M HAVING SEX WITH A BOY!' Next, I went to a one-on-one tutorial in which my poor professor enthused about Richard Martin's crazed heavenly scenes.[4] I couldn't hear a word because my mind was ablaze. An internal voice shouted, 'OH, MY GOD! I JUST FUCKED A BOY! I JUST FUCKED A BOY!' I was so excited I almost told him.

I had a boyfriend. *I had a fucking boyfriend!* He was adorable, strange and polite, and delighted to have me, too. He laughed at my jokes and looked after me when I was ill. I'd set my alarm in the middle of the night so I could wake up and think, There he is. This is my boyfriend. He's in bed with me. With me!

The sex had novelty value, but that didn't last – we were always the same people, doing the same things in the same place. A few times Jack struggled to make things more interesting, but he was fighting a losing battle: I didn't want anal, I liked lying down – and I wanted my home comforts, too. After a couple of scratchy incidents in North Wales and the New Forest, I vetoed outdoor sex.

---

4 Richard Martin painted bizarre bombastic biblical epics full of clouds, angels, devils and ecstatic ascents to heaven.

Heavy Petting

You made me give you a blow-job in a field.
I didn't really want to but to save a fuss, I kneeled.
You wanted me to finish you without using my hands –
I had to scrunch my lips up tight just like a rubber band.

As I laboured on I felt my knees get damp.
Fifteen minutes into it my cheeks began to cramp.
You cried out, 'My God! Don't stop! I'm nearly there!'
I knew the worst was coming when you grabbed hold of my hair.

OH! Heavy petting in the great outdoors,
Caterpillars, ladybirds and dandelion spores,
Cold and wet, no privacy,
Doesn't sound like fun to me!

You made me fuck you in among the trees,
I didn't really want to but you kept on saying, 'Please',
Lying on a prickly patch alive with ants,
I was cold and petulant without my pants.

It was over quickly but then, oh, my cries
When I saw that I'd attracted half a dozen flies.
Leaping up, I grabbed my clothes and drove back home,
And that's where I've had sex since then; preferably alone.

OH! Heavy petting in the great outdoors,
Caterpillars, ladybirds and dandelion spores,
Cold and wet, no privacy,
Doesn't seem like fun to me!

Hmmm, sex. I quite liked it when it was going on, but I'd always need a drink to get remotely worked up, which insulted Jack and pissed me off. I thought he was totally gorgeous, so why didn't my body react? I put it down to inhibition and my old standby: something was wrong with me. Also, now that I was ensconced in a relationship, all the longing faded away, and sex never crossed my mind unless it was happening. It was like the jam in a doughnut – the sticky, messy bit that came wrapped in lovely sweet dough. A typical post-coital scene looked something like this:

'Chief, where did you put my knickers?'

'Huh?'

'You know, sex is like violin practice: I have a hard time getting started. I can't be bothered, and then afterwards I feel like it was worth the effort, and I'm, like, "Hmm. I should really do that more often . . ." So I'm sorry . . . Jack?'

He'd already be asleep. This kind of activity took a lot out of him, and a twenty-four-hour post-coital depression would inevitably descend.

And so, things pootled pleasantly along until he went mad. When he stopped being mad we ended up in London, like everybody else, living first in a vicarage, then on a council estate and, finally, in our own flat in a mansion block infested with homeless drug addicts. We got easy, silly jobs writing nonsense, and hung out with my friends after work. About five years on, everything was trundling along nicely, but there wasn't much magic in the air. I was a freelance recruitment copywriter, stuck in the armpit of the advertising industry. I used my wits for the powers of evil, luring people into unappealing jobs. And, for some reason, I felt sad as soon as I had any free time. Our flat was infested with mould, insects scurried through the gaps, the electrician said we'd die if we used the shower, but the sports centre had only one hot one and that was marked 'disabled'. The day a disabled person banged on the door, I realized I'd had it with London. I walked back through the frost, marched into the bedroom and shoved Jack's toe.

'Chief,' I said, 'wake up. I want to get married.'

I had a plan: we'd go to San Francisco and ride the dot-com boom with our friends Tim and Tina (T&T). My friend Ben handled fish-fingers and sanitary towels at a fancy product agency in Soho: if I wanted a sexy job like that, I knew I had to move to where the economy was exploding. The Great Move would also salve my travel complex. The Brontës had done OK stuck in Yorkshire; my grandparents would never have left Scotland even if they'd had the chance; my parents thought going to France was an adventure. But expectations had changed, and my lack of international experience had become a source of embarrassment. By the time my thirtieth birthday was just visible with the naked eye, if you squinted hard at the horizon, it seemed I'd missed the boat, the bus and the plane. I was surrounded by well-travelled friends with great photo collections, and all I'd notched up were several trips to Europe, mostly gloom-laden, including a waterlogged French hitch-hiking trip that triggered my worst cold sores ever. I'd also spent three weeks with a youth orchestra in New England, where my host – a forty-seven-year-old refrigerator salesman – had taken to waking me up by stroking my forearm. He followed me to Boston airport and sent love-letters for months, culminating in an offer to leave his wife. 'Abroad' seemed a dangerous place. I didn't want to go anywhere, I just wished I'd already *been*.

But if I *lived* abroad, it wouldn't be 'abroad' any more. What I needed was a Significant Change of Address.

Jack agreed to my proposal. I would now be officially, legally secure. 'Chief,' I said, 'I really like belonging to someone, don't you? Chief?'

'Mmmm.'

I was surprised that the M-word tasted so delicious. We were being very pragmatic about it, but we did love each other, and . . .

well, I glowed when I thought about it. It would have been nice if Jack had asked me, but I felt honoured to be licensed to reproduce with a man of such noble bearing: with his perfect skin, vision and teeth, and no allergies, he was in the fast lane of the gene pool.

We visited my parents to break the good news. They were delighted by the M-word. 'Marriage is a promotion for any woman!' beamed Dad, who wrote a cheque for a thousand pounds on the spot.

Mum was equally unequivocal: 'Congratulations!'

I was glad that she wasn't upset – but why the hell wasn't she upset? Her only daughter, her closest friend and confidante, the only person she could argue with properly, was moving to the other side of the world. 'Congratulations'?

The next day, I found her weeping in the downstairs loo. I put my arm round her shoulders. 'What's wrong, Mum?'

'Nothing, darling.' She sniffed. 'Mother's all right.'

'Are you upset about me going away?'

'Oh, my darling, I didn't want you to see me like this. I'm going to miss you, of course, but this is a marvellous opportunity for you both and Mother wants the very best for you. You go for it, my darling!' *Sniff.*

'I don't want you to be sad, Mum.' I knew she would be, though. I was about to embark upon a grand, transatlantic guilt trip.

Sadly, Jack wasn't so keen on the sentimentality. 'I was thinking,' he said, one day, 'this wedding, it's sort of lying.'

'S'pose so,' I muttered.

'Isn't it, Lins?'

I staunched the hurt with practicalities. 'Do you want to return all the cheques, then?'

Two months later, Jack and I flew out to see if we liked San Francisco. We stayed with T&T, my dot-com friends. The sun was shining, and there was an English grocery opposite, so we gave it the thumbs-up and booked a wedding for Friday afternoon. Though

Mum had initially been upset about me getting married overseas, threatening to book flights for the whole family, 5,500 miles proved an effective deterrent. I couldn't see myself playing the princess in a family drama: I didn't look the part, and we hated being together, so what was the point of all that razzmatazz and expense? My dad wasn't arguing. So, the day after I turned twenty-seven, Jack and I tied the knot in a sweet and minimal way, witnessed by T&T, plus a party of Japanese schoolchildren on a guided tour about seismic retro-fitting. You don't get City Hall to yourself for nineteen dollars.

We dressed up for the occasion: I wore Miss New Zealand's dress from the finals of Miss Universe 1989[5] and Jack teamed a suit with a partridge tie. And the glamour didn't end there: our wedding night was spent in the luxury suite of the Santa Cruz Econolodge (eighty-three dollars, plus tax), with our two friends. After dinner, we smuggled three bottles of champagne into the hotel pool, splashing ourselves silly then weaving back to the suite, where Jack fell headlong into the master bedroom. I climbed on to the couch with T&T, who had switched on the Shopping Channel. 'What are you doing, Lins?' Tim grinned. 'You should be getting in there!'

'He was talking about consummation,' I muttered, and Tina passed me a cushion. Soon the peaceful snores of my new/old husband were wafting through the plasterboard partition and I left my friends to their fat-busting machines and limited-edition hand-painted porcelain dolls.

'Goodnight.'

A couple of days later Jack and I flew back to London and started the visa-application process. After nine months of tedium, the US Embassy told us that, while our massive stack of paperwork was in order, I couldn't have a Green Card unless Jack had a US address and a job that paid more than $22,000 a year. While he sorted that out, I had to stay in the UK.

5 I had inadvertently befriended a beauty queen.

Separation was a daunting prospect, but I was determined not to give up. I told Jack when to resign from his London job, booked his flight, gave notice on the flat, and made plans to stay with friends for a couple of weeks while he picked up a job in the US.

Then he had flown away to become my stars-and-stripes-crossed lover. Every few days he'd call me. Our conversations were always the same.

'I miss you, Bun.'

'I miss you, too.'

'I wish you were here, Bun.'

'I wish I was, too.'

'I miss making love with you, Bun.'

'I miss, um, you, too.'

2: Them and Us

'There are a lot of idiots in this world.'

Mum

'Hi, Linda . . .'s Jack! 'S OK . . . I've prob'ly godda place . . .'s OK, m'Bun. Carn talkboudit now . . .'s OK, luv you!'

Jack had been in San Francisco for three months when he found a place. It was a depressing shit-hole full of annoying clowns, but it was his. That filthy den was to be the perfect backdrop to our decaying love.

When, after a long and increasingly desperate search, he got a job, I was legally able to join him. I had to have three vaccinations, an AIDS test and a TB X-ray; I got the all-clear. I got on the plane, off the plane, on another plane, and seventeen hours later, stumbled into San Francisco airport, laden with musical instruments and ready for my new life in the sun.

As I rolled my luggage cart through the double doors, I saw my long-lost husband leaning against a pillar, wearing a familiar brown shirt and a gentle smile. 'Hello!' he said. We shared a hug and lots of little kisses, and he steered us to the taxi rank, one arm round me, the other on my luggage mountain.

I'd played out this moment endlessly in my mind, complete with trumpet fanfare and fireworks, but now that it was real, it felt strangely normal to see him. I checked, and he felt the same way. How could it be so prosaic? I plumped for an answer that felt good:

'I think we're back where we belong, Chief, so why should it be exciting to come home?'

He tightened his grip on my shoulders. 'That's right, Bun.'

I was in our bedroom, unpacking my accordion. 'Listen to this!' I launched into a halting rendition of 'Jingle Bells'.

'That's great, Bun! Can we have sex now?'

'Don't you want to hear "Over the Waves"? I can almost do it without stopping.'

'I've got vodka in the freezer!' He ran off to get me a shot, then proffered it across my heaving bellows. I stopped playing, unstrapped myself and drank up. It felt good to be held again. Oh, yes! I thought. Sex is nice, isn't it? Why did I always forget?

'Oh, my Bun,' sighed Jack afterwards, drifting into a sleepy miasma. 'It's so great to have you back. I can't wait to show you off to everyone tomorrow.'

I lay beside him in the dark, wide awake. Fuck. I was here. I'd made it all happen. The car engine had stopped, but this time the melancholy of arrival was tinged with wicked relief, as if I'd avoided cleaning up after a wild party by running away at dawn. Now I couldn't look after Mum.

The next morning I began to meet my new housemates. Let's start at the front of the house and work our way back.

Main bedroom
In the bed
Name: Kyle
Age: 25
Appearance: pulled-up knee socks with shorts
Philosophy: evangelical Christian
Source: Texas
Occupation: art student
Manner: silent but creepy

Liked:
- picking up short women and throwing them on to soft surfaces
- lube samples
- painting dark splodges evocative of unbearable suffering
- tinned pears
- sniggering about boobs after dark

On the floor
Name: Mike
Age: 42
Appearance: short, fat and hairy
Philosophy: evangelical Christian (same church)
Source: Texas (same town)
Occupation: sound engineer for touring production of *Les Misérables*
Manner: jovial
Liked:
- curry
- snoring
- large boobs

Back bedroom *(back half of the double parlour. In auditory terms, the same room)*
Name: Jack
Age: 25
Appearance: tall, handsome, etc.
Philosophy: BA/it rains for a reason
Source: Wales and America
Occupation: copywriter/misanthropic poet
Manner: plodding, well-intentioned
Liked:
- dogs

- British punk music 1978–83
- anal sex (aspirationally)
- vodka (liberally)
- cigarettes (nostalgically)
- me (emphatically)

Bathroom
Well-established conurbations of four billion-plus, devastated by surprise attack of UK origin

---

Hallway
Name: Tova
Age: 24
Appearance: travelling girl
Philosophy: I want therefore I get
Source: Canada
Occupation: boat-hand/self-promoter
Manner: upfront and annoying
Liked:
- sex
- travelling
- talking about sex and travelling
- rice
- yoga
- shouting in Spanish to her boyfriend, (who emerged, cockroach-style, as soon as she'd secured the 'room')

Name: Chico
Age: 34
Appearance: small, brown, hardened
Philosophy: Tova wants, therefore I get it for her
Source: Chile
Occupation: boat-hand and burger-flipper

Manner: benign or confused, maybe both

Liked:

- sex
- travelling
- rice
- yoga
- his sister (they'd recently ended a long-term, live-in relationship)

Kitchen

Name: The miserable boy who lives in the kitchen

Age: *c.* 20

Appearance: lank

Philosophy: why?

Source: America

Occupation: lying on the couch reading academic books about torture, death, prostitution

Manner: limp

Liked:

- fraternizing with the landlord's arch enemy, which led to him being punched in the face, thrown out of the kitchen and chased up the street by the landlord, who was driving a truck

---

Utility nook

Name: Richard

Age: 28

Appearance: fuzz-headed loon with too many teeth

Philosophy: whatever, dude!

Source: Oregon

Occupation: skateboarder, thief

Manner: insane

Liked:

- skateboarding

- TV
- pizza
- a sixteen-year-old girl whom he had to return – drunk, unconscious and splattered with her own vomit – to her grandmother
- yelling inanities

Our 'landlord' was also an official resident, and the most interesting of the lot. He was one of many parasitical entrepreneurs shot to power by the dot-com boom. As people fought for space and rents tripled, he moved in with his girlfriend and illegally sublet his dingy flat to the drifters, thieves and unemployed copywriters no one else wanted. It was a sort of for-profit charity. To ward off the usual avalanche of responses, he posted vacancy ads like this:

Small hallway available
No Christians

The place was full of his crap, and every so often he popped 'home' to fuss about bills and pick up a volume of intellectual erotica. He'd caused a scandal at the art college with a performance piece involving an enema – a quick Google told me he'd found a student volunteer, got him to sign a waiver, tied him up, extracted shit from the volunteer's backside, and then from his own, exchanged the faecal matter using an enema, fellated the volunteer and exited to a smattering of polite applause. Next he was expelled, and six months later he was still recoiling from the shock.

'Honestly, Linda,' he said, out of the blue, 'he was into it at the time!'

I put down my sandwich. 'Who was?'

'That bastard kid!'

'You mean the one you did the enema stuff to?'

'Yeah! But when the story went national, they all changed their tune. He lodged a formal complaint against me, coz he was afraid of lookin' like a pervert! Some sponsor got antsy so they used me as a scapegoat. They banned me from campus! I feel kind of betrayed, you know?'

The affair had turned him to drink, but it was hard to tell, as he claimed to be a professional wine-taster. Surrounded by charts of Italian grape regions, empty wine crates and magazine racks bulging with copies of *Connoisseur*, he liked to shoogle a huge wine glass, saying, 'Mmmm . . .' In fact, his experience was limited to two months on the till at Quoit Liquors, and he was currently un-employed. His identity in crisis, he made a big deal of his friendship with Steve Labash, a performance artist and high priest in the Church of Satan, whose best-known protest piece involved him being naked with a bottle of whisky:

1. Smash the neck off a whisky bottle.
2. Slash your skin with the raw edge.
3. Pour the rest of the whisky over your wounds.

But all the enemas, devil-worship and lit-porn in the world couldn't conceal his darkest secret: he was nice.

A card had already arrived from home.

Dear Linda, just your old mum writing to say hello. I found this postcard from when we were in the Isle of Wight – Dad tripped up in the mud, remember? Look after yourself, my darling; I've got to run to catch the post, lots of love,
Mum XXX

Back in the present, things weren't so sweet. Jack would leave for work every morning, and I'd have a lonely day to fill. By late afternoon, I might have visited the ironmonger's three times – it's amazing how many things you don't realize you need until you're really bored. I was becoming a familiar face to the strange man behind the counter. 'Your total is sixteen-oh-nine!' He beamed. 'I love your accent. Australia, right?'

I reached for my rubber-footed cheese-grater. 'England.'

'Well, close, eh?'

'Not really.'

'English, eh? There are some great Irish bars around here. We should go out for a drink some time.'

'Mm . . . yeah.' I looked down into my purse. I wasn't used to this kind of talk. I'd never been on a date.

'Yeah,' he pressed on, 'like Jimmy Foley's and the Green Giant. You know them?'

'No,' I said. 'Well, see you!'

As soon as I was out of the door, I broke into a run. This meant I couldn't go into the hardware shop any more. Damn it. I was so bored it seemed like a loss. This wasn't how I'd envisaged the Golden State. The laws of gravity still applied: it was just plain old reality, minus my friends. Admittedly, the weather was better, and I found all kinds of reasons to go outside. I walked up and down perilously tilted pavements, each block affording me another fabulous sea-and-sky-filled view, buildings tumbling together, nestling in valleys and skimming hilltops as though they were on the crest of a wave. The air was warm and breezy, rich with ions, and its touch on my skin was a pleasure. On cloudy days the locals moaned, while I gasped at the mist – chunks of cloud suspended in the air like scenery in a divine school play. But however beautiful my surroundings, I didn't belong there.

I confided in Jack: 'It makes me so angry, Chief. I have you, and that's just the most amazing thing, and I'm still sad. Why can't I just be happy?'

'That's what you always say, and you never are. To be honest, I don't think you ever will be.'

38

So I went to the doctor and told her I'd been feeling a bit blue. Without blinking, she wrote me repeat prescriptions for a thousand Prozac capsules. 'You should be feeling better in about three weeks.' I read that the side-effects included lower libido and increased homicidal urges.

As I made dinner, Tova would sidle in and tell me about her amazing life – the places she'd been, the people she'd met and the wild things she'd done. She could make anything dull, but next to this vigorously sprouting shrub, I felt like a limp, etiolated stem. To protect myself, I responded only to direct probes, such as 'You're from England, right?'

'Yup.'

'Hmm. Where else have you lived?'

'Here.'

'Just here? Well, where have you been, like long trips?'

'Nowhere.'

'Oh . . . Really?'

'Really.'

She was all about the where, not the what. I couldn't stand her, and boycotted the kitchen when she was around. Jack would come home from work to find me sitting on the bed with an open can of tuna and a bag of crisps.

'Here's dinner, Chief.'

'Lins, can't you at least make some pasta?'

'No,' I said. 'I'll have to talk to Tova while it boils.'

'Well, you turn on the water, then I'll go in a bit and sort it out.'

I agreed, but she caught me in the hall and pointed at my pink socks. 'Look, Chico!' she cried, laughing. 'They match her sweater!' I was a pink moth, writhing on a pin. 'Ah, yes,' she said, 'I used to do that – match stuff. When I was much younger, of course.'

I reversed back into our room. 'Jack,' I hissed, 'we have to get out of this place! I can't stay indoors in the daytime because it's like a dungeon and it makes me feel really sad and I can't go outdoors because there's nothing left to buy and I'm getting sunburned and

I can't stay indoors at night because I'm going to kill Tova and I can't go out at night because there's nowhere to go because I don't have any friends.'

'Let's go for a walk,' said Jack. 'We can get some food, too.'

We clambered to the top of Lombard Street, a giant game of crazy-golf, twisting and turning down towards the mass of the city. Beyond the clustered lights lay the black expanse of the bay, and beyond that more land, more lights, more people, doing more interesting things than I was. It was time to confront the truth: I was not a writer, because writers write stuff.

'Chief,' I wailed, sitting down, 'I'm just, like – nothing! And my face is all bumpy.'

It was true: I'd got a weird sort of rash. He patted my head. 'It's OK, you're still the best rabbit in the world!'

My tears blurred the city into a twinkling puddle. 'I'll never write anything except recruitment ads!'

Jack held me close. 'That's OK, Bun. I'll still love you more than anything in the world and I'd love you if you couldn't even write your own name.' He cradled my head in his lap and wiped my tears on his shirtsleeve. 'Poor Bun. You've got mascara all over your face.'

Comforted, I grew calmer. We had a few minutes of silence while he stroked my hair. 'It's OK.' I sniffed. 'You know, I feel kind of a sense of relief. Denying it all this time, when it's fine not to write stuff. Who cares?'

'Well, maybe you don't need it to be my lovely Bun, but you might need it to be a happy, fulfilled rabbit.'

How annoying. Not just the herbivore references – he wouldn't let me off the hook. All of a sudden I had an idea. I sat up, still sniffing. 'I know! I could write about all the freaks I meet here!'

He squeezed my hand. 'That's a great idea. You've got all this time, Bun, and you've not had it for years. You deserve to put it to good use. If nothing else, it'll make you feel better. You can write short stories.'

'Can't do anything that long.'

'Poems, then.'

'Nobody reads poems except other poets.'

'Hmm.'

'What if I stuck a tune on top? Then they'd be songs. And maybe a few people will listen.' I'd written a song once, to promote the use of dustbins on school premises. I was back on track, so we got some dinner, and then returned to the house, where Jack immediately conducted a bottom inspection. It was a new habit of his, and it got on my nerves.

'Hmm, let's see. Turn round.' He put his hands inside my knickers and started feeling around. 'Oh, it's been trimmer – it's been trimmer! You'll have to keep hopping up those hills, Bun!' Soon his hands were round my waist, then inside my shirt, and he seemed to have forgotten about my below-par backside. 'I love you, Bun.'

'I love you too, Chief.'

Lips met and tongues coiled together as he began to unpeel my skirt; my clothes always seemed to be falling off when Jack was around. Suddenly he disengaged. 'Hey,' he said, 'I've got an idea.'

'What?'

'Let's do it standing up.'

'What? No.'

'Well, how about the other way, then? It feels nice, you know. I stuck that corn-on-the-cob up my arse and it was . . . you know . . . It felt good.'

I was sick of hearing about that damned thing, a plastic corn-on-the-cob vibrator we'd been given as a wedding present. I'd thrown it out after he'd claimed repeatedly to have stuck it up his butt. 'Jack,' I said, 'I still don't believe you did it. Or with the wine bottle.'

'I did it! It was just the spout. Why don't you believe me? Why would I lie?'

'Look, Jack, I'm not having anal sex with you.'

'So let's do it standing up, then. Go on!'

'No.'

'Christ, Lins, you're so boring.' He went to bed in a huff, his face turned towards the wall. What was going on? He'd never asked for stuff like that when we were in London.

I spent much of the next day working out a song on my accordion. When Jack got home from work, he hugged me and the accordion, and asked if we could have sex standing up.

'No.'

'You can take the accordion off.'

'No.'

'Please, Lins. We always do it lying down.'

'I like lying down. Why do something standing up when you can do it lying down?'

'Go on.'

'I want to play you my song.'

He stepped back and crossed his arms. 'Go on, then.'

My Landlord is a Pervert

My landlord doesn't live here, and that's a piece of luck
Coz he isn't very fussy about what he likes to fuck.
My landlord is a pervert, and that's all right with me,
He keeps the house in order, and sometimes stays for tea.

He keeps his books at our place – philosophical texts,
Nietzsche, Kant and Hegel on the ins and outs of sex.
My landlord is a pervert, and that's all right with me,
He keeps the house in order, and sometimes stays for tea.

He is awfully fond of enemas and he does them in the park,
Finds an unsuspecting vagrant and makes his muddy mark.[6]

6 I made that bit up.

My landlord is a pervert, and that's all right with me,
He keeps the house in order, and sometimes stays for tea.

He is best friends with a male prostitute and a Satanist called Steve,
They hang out in hard-core nightclubs with sailors on shore leave.
My landlord is a pervert, and that's all right with me,
He keeps the house in order, and sometimes stays for tea!

'That's great, Bun! So, can we do it standing up?'

'No.'

'Please.'

'I'll get cold.'

'Go on – put your wedding shoes on and then you'll be tall enough.'

He was starting to get snotty, and I couldn't stand being frozen out. 'Back in a sec,' I said, and trotted off to the kitchen for a swig of vodka. The wedding shoes were six-inch platforms with black leather ankle straps. I did up all the little thongs and wobbled to a precarious upright.

'Christ, Lins.' He grinned. 'You're so fuckable! Stand up! There you go. See, we're nearly the same height now so we can do it like this. It'll fit.'

I felt horribly exposed without a bed on one side of me, like a giant whiting fillet. The 3-D nudity was especially awkward in those ridiculous shoes. And how was I supposed to come? I couldn't twiddle myself to a climax with Jack in the way. Still, it was probably worth it; otherwise he'd be a grumpy sod. Five more minutes, I told myself, and I'd be back on the bed, reading my book.

'Bend your knees a bit, Bun.'

I assumed the don't-get-pee-on-your-shoes position while he shoved, blindly.

'Help me, then, Lins. A bit of guidance, for God's sake.'

I sighed. 'Is this going to happen every time I wear these shoes?'

He oiled the machinery with spit and tried again. 'Aah, that's it.' *Uuup down up down up down up down up down up down up down up down up ...* My shoulder-blade kept knocking against the door jamb. And I *was* cold.

The best thing about fucking was that I got to lie down.

3: Work

'You've got to have enough money. That's the most important thing.'

Mum

If I'd held on to my career, it would have been easier to hold on to Jack. But who was I to make the rules when he made all the money?

As much as he despised his new job, he liked his new workmates: 'They're such a great bunch, Lins!' Their interests ranged from drinking and smoking to talking in funny accents. They bonded through cigarettes, which had been Jack's comfort since he was ten years old. After gargantuan efforts, I'd had him off them for a few months, but his new colleagues thought that true friends die together, and invited him for a smoke five or six times a day. Eventually, his resolve cracked and they initiated him into the gang with a flaming lighter. To his delight, he was then automatically included in the after-lunch pot-smoking sessions. He kept on telling me how cool they were, once you got to know them.

'Mmm,' I said.

'They're so social and loyal – it's amazing.'

'Mmm. Do they ever see anybody from outside of work?'

'Well, they spend every Friday or Saturday night together, at any rate. I guess it's pretty incestuous, though. Like, there's this tarty account-handler whom everyone fancies, called Gayle – she's really sweet, she's got an amazing arse, you have to see it, she's kind of pudgy but really cute-looking – and I thought it was just kind of light-hearted, but some of them are deadly serious about it. They're fighting over her!'

'Really? Who's going to win?'

'No one. She's really smart. Dressing like that and acting flirty gets her what she wants, but I don't think she'll do it with any of them. They're dying of frustration, but no one will actually ask her out.'

'Do you fancy her?'

'No, not really. Well, to be honest, I just want to fuck her up the arse.'

While Jack's anal-sex fixation grew ever more intense and while – unbeknown to me – our relationship was careening towards the rocks, I remained jobless and increasingly desperate to get out of the house. I'd gaze at the towers downtown, speckled with a million windows, a million ways in, thinking that somewhere, in all of that, there had to be a little space for me. I longed to find a job, but I'd never had much luck in that department. After all, back in London, I'd worked in recruitment advertising.

What the fuck is 'recruitment advertising'?

In London, you're never more than eight feet away from a rat or a recruitment advertisement. This clandestine industry operates under the radar of normal human awareness, like the Masons without the handshakes and the (alleged) sex parties. Here's what's going on: some crap companies struggle to find good staff, others to find any staff at all. Instead of increasing salaries or improving working conditions, they prefer to spend their money on tailor-made propaganda with which to ensnare unsuspecting candidates. And that's where the recruitment ad agency comes in. It's not a field that anyone aims to get into, and this was how it happened to me:

In 1995, I graduated with no useful skills. I guarded books in the library of a stately home (where my parents discovered me asleep on the job, sitting upright in a chair), cleaned toilets and made coffee. I then worked on the till in Boots, tended a bar and worked in a cake shop – a nightmare for anyone with a potentially fatal allergy to eggs. In the new year, I went to Liverpool to volunteer in an arts centre for poor kids, where I learned that poor kids were scary. The centre was an unheated church, which was so viciously cold that I chose to run a bake-your-name-in-a-biscuit class, the lure of the oven outweighing the stress of working with eggs. Fifty hours a week I was embroiled in some farcical activity or other, entitling me to a mattress in an unheated, dusty attic. This was winter in the north of England. There was snow on the ground. I washed my jumper, hung it to dry in the basement and returned three weeks later to find it wetter than ever. No one ever took off their clothes except to have a bath. Three months of this was enough to give me some kind of lung disease, so Mum and Dad drove up to rescue me.

Next, I went to France with Jack, where I contracted chicken-pox, and ended up back with my parents, covered with pink spots. When I was up and about again, I got a job as a pizza waitress, and discovered too late that the uniform had short sleeves. I tried to cover up my arm scabs with concealer, but lasted only a day. Then I decided to go abroad, but an intensive Teaching English as a Foreign Language (TEFL) course took me no further than south London. Teaching English to Italians in Tooting (TEIT) was a three-hours-a-day gig that involved six trains, and I was fired before the summer ended.

All this time, I'd been applying for bottom-of-the-rung jobs in anything connected with words. Dozens of applications had resulted in just two interviews, both of which I'd mucked up by speaking with unrelenting sarcasm in a tremulous whisper. Eventually I realized I'd have to work for nothing, and condescended to contact the editorial departments of various magazines. To my surprise, they had all filled their slave-labour quotas, so I targeted the picture desks instead, hoping to get a toe in the door. My first 'yes' was from *Tatler*, so that was where I started. I didn't know that it was a society-'n'-shopping rag for the landed gentry. Too late, I found myself knee deep in cashmere pashminas with matching handbags. For full-time grunt work, I got travel expenses, plus three pounds a day for lunch, which nicely plumped out my thirty-nine-pounds-a-week dole money. (Mum was taking care of my rent – twenty pounds a week for a mattress on the floor in a vicarage.) On my first day at the swanky office I wore a red wool dress I'd picked up in Portobello market. 'I don't believe it!' neighed the editor. 'A work-experience girl who knows how to dress!'

The magazine operated like a feudal society, in which the ideas came from half a dozen posh people, with unnervingly white teeth, who passed on the labour to an army of unemployed graduates. While we toiled away, the skeleton staff (no joke, they were all anorexic or dying to look it) spent their days blabbing on the phone, chewing salad leaves or getting their teeth polished. A typical day involved traipsing to New Bond Street to pick up a £5000 Loewe suitcase for a photo-shoot, then spending three hours on the phone fact-checking an insultingly vague, scrawled wish-list of dream luggage for winter skiing holidays.

But as those three excruciating months drew to a close, I was filled with dread. Worse was to come: I was scheduled for six weeks on the picture desk at *Vogue*. I'd been up there on various errands, and everyone had matching belts and nails, and pointy shoes that cost at least thirty pounds per toe. Every night I prayed to the media gods: 'Please, let me get a job before I have to go to *Vogue*.' In between, I had a placement at *i-D* magazine, the po-faced style bible for urban hipsters. Everyone was fashionable *and* cool. Because they weren't fake, they weren't friendly. The art director was indifferent, unshaven, and seemed surprised to see me. 'I suppose you could do some photocopying,' he mumbled. In desperation, I went to the loo, but I couldn't get back into the office as I didn't know the door code. Trapped in a cold, echoing corridor, I lost it. I ran from the building in a flood of tears. Hysterical, I phoned Mum, who listened sympathetically and advised me to catch the first train home.

And then the unthinkable happened – I got an interview. The job title was 'journalist'. With glam mags on my CV, I felt it was within my grasp. This feeling was waning a week after the interview, when Jack decided to take action. He sat me on his lap and said firmly, 'Now, Bun, call that bitch and tell her why you're the best person for the job.'

'I can't. I'll look desperate.'

'Lins, you *are* desperate. Do it.'

'What if I'm not the best person for the job?'

'You are. Course you are. Now do it. Call her now. I'm right behind you.'

He held me tight, and I made myself do it, earning a big kiss and – after my trial period – eleven grand a year.

Eleven grand! It seemed a lot of money until I tried to live on it.

My new boss *was* a bitch. A smiley bitch with a fake laugh and bad suits. This tousle-haired Medusa barked orders in threes, and sneered when I asked her to repeat, so I'd go round asking people to guess what she wanted. 'OK, here are the clues: umbrellas, under the window and Prince Albert.' I'd walk round the block waiting for the tears to stop, hide in the loo or take refuge in the storage cupboard (where, contrary to office lore, I was discovered asleep only once). My job title was misleading: the place sold pictures, and I wrote the accompanying text, which helped sell the snaps, but rarely got published alongside them. I would whiz through my daily batch of fashion and celebrity snaps, then get to work on old stock – pictures of homing pigeons or the Queen Mother's ready-to-run obituary. To break the tedium, I took down my trousers and modelled a fart-filter (my rear later appeared in a Swedish magazine), and interviewed a corporate shaman, who sat in the office burning sage while we danced to her drumbeat, snickering. I was sent out to interview a man who had been sexy in 1962.

I soon jumped ship and landed in the West End, next to the BBC HQ and the flagship branch of Top Shop, in the dark heart of recruitment advertising. My colleagues were all male, witty and self-deprecating. It was the first place where I felt I belonged to the gang, and our day-long banter detracted marvellously from the demoralizing work. Together we filled our days with useful activities: one tapped away at a screenplay laid out on his monitor to look like ad copy; others stood by the window, spotting stars going in and out of the BBC building, before joining the head of copy at the Dog and Pickle around noon. Later in the day we'd make paper costumes or throw things at each other, running up ads whenever there was a lull in activity.

My favourite client was Sun Valley, a chicken-processing plant in Yorkshire. Sun Valley was a great place to work for three reasons:

1. You got paid.
2. You got a free pair of rubber gloves and a hat.
3. You might not have to deal with giblets.

It was my job to convince unemployed locals that this was a marvellous career opportunity. I churned out dozens of variations on a feathered theme: *Your beak break! Give us a wing!* Our boss, the creative director, would descend unpredictably from his penthouse, and pace about, making us all nervous. One day, after I'd been there a couple of months, he leaned over my shoulder and said gently, 'Could we have a word?' I followed him into a small, cold room with no windows, where we sat down. 'Linda,' he said, 'it's been noticed that you leave work at five p.m. almost every day.'

'Yes,' I acknowledged. 'That's what's on my contract.'

'Ye-e-s,' he said, 'but it's supposed to be a *minimum*.'

'But I've always got my work done when I leave.'

'Ye-e-s, but is it done to the best of your abilities? It's about giving one hundred and ten per cent here. So, this weekend, I want you to ask yourself if you really want to work here at Jobfab.'

I was stunned. Nobody did a stroke of work after five. It was all right for the boys, but could I really stand another eight hours a week of indoor cricket, *Tomb Raider* and free beer?

On Monday afternoon, I met up again with my boss. I'd spent the morning in the loo with stress-induced diarrhoea, and I had nothing left to lose. 'So, Linda,' he began, 'did you think about what we said?'

I nodded. 'I guess I'm not as committed as the rest of the creative department.' He made a 'yes, indeed' face. 'I mean,' I said, 'you can tell that straight off from my *Tomb Raider* rating.'

'*Tomb Raider?*'

'Face it, my score's way below the others. I'm no good at cricket, and I can't drink half as much beer.'

'So . . . ?'

'So what I'm saying is, I think it would be best for everyone if I left, and tripled my income by freelancing at other agencies.'[7]

'Now, hold on, Linda, let's not—'

And thus began the next stage of my career:

Linda Robertson
Nomadic Copywriter
nomadcopy@bullshit.co.uk
Exorbitant rates * No job too risible

---

7 This is my fantasy rendering of what I would have said, had I been incredibly cool.

This led to the same old rubbish, but at three times the pay. I'd sit in gloomy offices with sagging ceiling tiles, waiting for an account-handler to brief me on how to promote pest-control jobs with Hackney Council. I photocopied novels so they looked work-related, and read my way through the long, grey days, taking grotesquely extended lonely lunch breaks.

That was the past, and Tina was taking care of the future, right here in San Francisco. She got me an interview at her marketing agency, Think! 'They're all Mormons,' she explained, 'but they're OK. Except David . . . He's – well, you'll see.'

David Aarse was her boss, and two weeks after my arrival in the city I found myself perched next to him on the San Francisco waterfront, blinking in the dazzling white light. The bay shimmered blue and white, and a fresh breeze tickled my arms. It was like having an interview in heaven – if this kept up, I'd get a tan. I took a deep, refreshing breath and turned to face my interrogator. The sun glowed like a halo through the bleached remnants of his hair, and black shades masked his eyes. As he flicked through my embarrassing portfolio, he muttered: 'Crap . . . crap . . . crap . . . Art direction's terrible . . . Now, that one's OK . . .' I tried to begin my spiel, but each time, he held up a silencing palm and flicked on through the book. Then, suddenly, he snapped it shut. 'Well,' he said, 'you can't write, but I like your accent. Linda, are you funny?'

'I *think*—'

'Don't think, do. That's the Think! motto. Listen, Linda, we're putting together an Internet movie, and we need an interviewer. Can you do it?'

'Um, yes,' I said, and cleared my throat. 'I was told fifty to seventy dollars an hour is the going rate.'

David turned his face to the sky. 'Well, Linda . . . I can only do twenty-five – an intern rate, I know, but it's going to be worth it. You see, we're in . . . what you might call an interesting situation.'

I asked him what he meant and he took a deep breath. 'Linda, we have no clients. That means we don't make any money. However, it offers huge creative freedom. Think! is a very exciting place to work right now. It's a true challenge.'

I accepted the challenge and the 75 per cent pay cut and returned home with a spring in my step – David Aarse wanted me Think!ing ASAP!

The very next morning I travelled purposefully downtown, gazing up at skyscrapers that jutted into flawless blue.

'I like your pants!' said a passer-by.

I reeled, and then I remembered: Americans talk to strangers; pants = trousers.

Soon I was gliding in a gold-plated lift to the Think! reception area, where a young woman sat reading a magazine in the shade of a gigantic, asymmetric blaze of tropical flowers. She looked up and smiled, gesturing for me to proceed. I found myself in a space the size of a football pitch, in which enough people to make up two teams swivelled listlessly in thousand-dollar ergonomic chairs. The place was heaving with the latest technology and the fridge was stocked with organic smoothies. I wondered vaguely who was funding all this, but then Tina came up and showed me round and I got distracted by all the activity. I was working on a website that would have been for Comedy Central TV if they'd commissioned it, but as they hadn't we had to keep it a secret in case they sued us for using their logo. The website spoofed the X Games[8] – taking place a few blocks down the road – using tiny skateboards and bicycles from cereal packets, and served to demonstrate the Think! flair. By the end of the day I had the Think! system pretty much worked out:

8 Extreme games – BMX, skateboarding, etc.

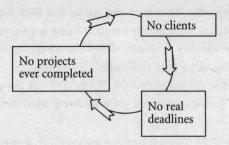

No clients

No projects ever completed

No real deadlines

A week later, I was standing on the pier in San Francisco, surrounded by X-treme sports fans with grey hoodies and outsize jeans melting over their sneakers. In my red polka-dot blouse, I felt like a cross between a clown and a traffic cone.

David Aarse interrupted my thoughts. He was preaching to his acolytes. 'A great creative solution isn't just about pretty pictures or witty strap lines. Never overlook the importance of the financial aspect. Because no business can operate on gloss alone.' He reached up to smooth his gleaming hair-nimbus. It was true: to demonstrate their business savvy to their non-existent clients, the Think! team would do anything – hang the expense! He turned to me. 'Now, see, Linda, this is what we're looking at . . .'

As far as I could tell, he wanted me to conduct hilarious interviews with skate-kids that would surreptitiously convey valuable data on the consumer habits of the target market sector. Under ideal conditions, I'd have struggled to build a rapport with them, and these conditions were far from ideal. For a start, David had decided that I wouldn't appear on camera: instead the on-screen interviewer would be a doll-head on a stick. I would crouch out of shot, addressing my questions to a knee.

'OK, Linda,' called David, 'we're rolling!' I cleared my throat and unfurled the question list, which kept flapping in the wind. Now, was there a question that wasn't too dreadful . . . ?

'Rolling!' said David, again.

'Um,' I said, to a flapping trouser-leg, 'why do you smell of tuna?'

'Whaaaah?'

David bent down. 'Linda, he can't hear you.'

I tried again. 'Why Do You Smell Of Tuna?'

'Whaaaah?'

Our cameraman turned to the kid: 'Sorry, man, she has an accent. The question is, why do you smell of tuna?'

'Whaddaya mean?'

I tried another tack. 'What Is Cool?' I shouted into the wind.

'What's cool? Oh, I dunno, like, skaters and stuff, you know? Like, the X Games! That's cool!'

Bingo! Time to slip in a marketing question. No one would ever notice. 'What was the last consumer durable you purchased?'

'Whaaaah?'

'What was the last thing you bought with a *plug* on it?'

My TV career proved short-lived, but as lay-offs weren't yet in vogue, David quietly demoted me to tagger-alonger. In my stead, he hired a dreadful little man who dressed up like a ladybird and went round hitting people with a balloon, all his own idea. I trudged around after them, slowly accruing my twenty-five dollars an hour. When the X Games drew to a close, I approached the Create! employment agency. 'Nothing today,' they chirped, 'but soon! Check in every day!'

Three weeks later, they dredged up something, and I went down-town to a swanky ad agency. There, a man with curly red hair sat me down and spoke as though we were planning an air raid. 'Thanks for coming in at the last moment, Linda.'

I tried to look as though I had something better to do. 'That's all right.'

'Excellent. So, here's the deal. Our client wants two options for this campaign, and we've already come up with the ideal solution.' He held up a drawing-pad with a blue scribble on it. I inspected 't and raised my eyebrows appreciatively. 'Nice . . .'

'Thanks,' he said. 'However, we need to offer them something else, something that's not so hot, so they get the impression they're *choosing* the ideal solution. And that's where you come in.'

I was confident that I could create something truly second-rate.

Next, Create! got me an interview for a permanent job with the brand-new interactive wing of a global ad agency. The creative director hired me on the spot. 'Great portfolio,' he said. 'Sharp. Edgy. I like it.' His judgement was awry, but I ran off a-sparkle, rushing into Jack's arms with the good news.

'Fifty bucks an hour?' He beamed. 'Full time? That's great!' He lifted me off my feet for an extra big hug. 'I'm so proud of you!'

'I'm so proud of me too!'

We went out to dinner to celebrate. 'You know,' he said, 'I really didn't want to come over here to San Francisco. And things have been pretty difficult so far. It was the worst time of my life, being here without you. But now I'm thinking that maybe we did the right thing after all.' He polished off his third whisky.

'I'm sorry I made you do it, Chief. I'm sorry I uprooted you from everything. I know you had a terrible time.'

'That's all right, Bun. We're together now and it's working out. Shall we get salmon-skin rolls? With little bits of lettuce for you?'

Things were looking up – we'd got ourselves a sun-drenched, overpriced pad with a palm-tree in the garden, and Jack was already bringing in enough to support us both. Viewing life as a ladder we couldn't fall off, we threw away our savings on designer sunglasses, roller-blades and CDs.

Sadly, life at the cutting edge of interactive advertising proved to be a lot like freelancing in London, except I couldn't get a single word approved. After two weeks I'd been given nothing to work on except the subject line for a single spam email.

- *See the potential. Reflect on your growth.*
- *A moment's reflection. A lifetime's growth.*
- *See your reflection; reach your potential.*
- *Your potential is reflected right here.*
- *Extraordinary potential. Time to reflect?*
- *Time to reflect on extraordinary potential.*

I passed my latest sheet to Slim, the head of copy. 'Yeah!' he said, nodding. 'Nice work! There are some really strong lines in here.'

'That's good,' I said, breaking a smile. 'I was beginning to think—'

'Yeah, you've nearly got it.'

'Nearly?'

'Yeah.'

My buttocks clenched inside my nice pants. 'So, um, how do I actually Get It?'

'Hmm.' He tapped his chin. 'I'd say . . . focus on the concept of "Extraordinary".'

I trudged back to my borrowed desk. Slumping in my ergonomic chair, I began to type yet again.

- *Reflect on extraordinary growth potential.*
- *Reflect on potential extraordinary growth!*
- *Reflecting extraordinary potential growth?*
- *Extraordinary potential: growth-reflecting.*
- *Extraordinary potential for reflecting growth.*
- *Potential growth reflecting the extraordinary.*
- *Growth potential reflecting the extraordinary.*
- *Extraordinary reflecting potential = growth!*
- *Grow extraordinary reflecting potential.*
- *Extraordinary! Reflect your growth potential.*
- *Potential: reflect your growth. Extraordinary!*
- *Reflect potential for growth: Extraordinary!*
- *Reflecting truth growing potenti . . .*

Why didn't they get a computer to generate this stuff? It wouldn't need its own ergonomic chair. I stood up and went to lunch.

As I ate my rice pudding, I calculated that if Slim ever accepted one of my sentences, it would have cost the company five hundred dollars a word. Considering this, I felt bad about downloading so many knitting patterns. It was time for some straight talk, so back at the office I collared the creative director.

'You're doing fine,' he purred, stroking his plastic hair. 'There's plenty of work. Just a bit sporadic. Start-ups.' Then he ducked into the loo.

The veneer began to disintegrate before my eyes, and I realized quickly that nobody else was doing any work either. Though the CEO kept making references to the future, he wouldn't give an exact date. We were 'temporarily' housed in a low-slung attic above a Chinese restaurant, with threadbare carpets and exposed wiring. Of course, we'd move into a marble palace ASAP, and I'd have my own ergonomic desk, chair and computer, but in the meantime would I mind squatting in the lobby over that big, dark stain? I stared out into the limitless azure beyond the murky windows, then followed my instincts and walked out.

As soon as I got home, I called Jack. 'I couldn't bear it any more, Chief. I told them where to stick it – under G for Goodbye. Actually, I said I had another job, which isn't really lying – it's referring optimistically to a future state. You don't mind, do you?'

'No, Bunny, I don't want you to suffer. No point us both having a stupid job that we hate. You'll get something much better.'

In fact, I didn't. There was no word from Create! and I began to give up hope. I started making elaborate food, reading French and lounging around the house a lot; things got so desperate that I started reading the paper. Not the news part, of course – just the column with the sex tips. 'A gentleman props himself up on his elbows,' it said. That was an option? I liked being squashed, but Jack was really heavy, and I couldn't breathe properly, and after a while the sweat made those farty sounds . . . But hang on, wasn't I supposed to be moaning, or something, sort of spontaneously? I just didn't have it in me, especially now that Prozac had me numb from the waist down. Oh, well, I suppose the occasional orgasm was a fair trade for the soft padding inside my skull. I put down the paper and got to work on a song, and by the time I'd finished, Jack came home with a bunch of irises. 'Hi, Bun!' he said. 'Writing a ditty?'

'Yup.'

'Great. What's it about?'

'That girl at work you want to fuck up the arse.'

'What – Gayle?'

'Yeah, it's about Gayle.'

'But you haven't met her.'

'I've seen her from a distance.'

'Let's hear it, then.'

'You might not like it.'

'I'm sure I'll like it. Go on.'

I cleared my throat.

All Made Up

Though her hair is blonde, she dyes it blonder,
Sticks plastic to her eyelids to make her lashes longer.
Her skin is almost perfect, though she covers it in crap,
She is carefully creating a reality gap.

Beneath it all, she's a natural girl,
Only pretending to be fake,
Trying to cope in a threatening world
And claim her share of the cake.

Though she is a good girl, she dresses like a whore.
It's good to leave your audience wanting more.

She covers up her shyness with ultra-padded bras,
Add two little bits of sponge and men start seeing stars.

Beneath it all, she's a natural chick,
Only pretending to be fake.
The hypocrisy of her life makes her sick
But there seems so much at stake!

Though naturally honest, she acts a little sly.
People seem to like it, she doesn't wonder why.
She really isn't stupid, but never lets it show,
Perhaps her mind is addled; her friends would never know.

Beneath it all, she's a natural dame,
Only pretending to be fake,
Thinks inside she is still just the same,
But she's making a big mistake.

Jack stood up and crossed his arms. 'That's really mean.'

'It's not mean, it's insightful.'

'Gayle's really cool.'

'No, she's not. She's a *faux*-tart.'

'I'm going out for a smoke.'

'You said you were going to stop. You promised.'

'Christ, leave me alone, would you?' He slammed the door behind him, and I sat down on the bed, ablaze with righteousness and embarrassment.

Back at work the next day, he sat in his office, having a think. Left alone in the US, he'd found himself a job, a home and even some new friends. The truth was, I wasn't actually *necessary*. This small but elemental groundshift had caused fissures to appear in our love, and as the relief of reunion ebbed away, they were becoming apparent. Were they structural, he wondered, or superficial? He took another toke on the office bong and Gayle tottered in. Her easy laugh, deft compliments and tight skirt helped him come to a conclusion, which he shared with me after we'd finished dinner that night. No point spoiling a good lasagne.

'That was lovely, Lins,' he said, clearing his plate. 'Listen, I've been thinking.'

'What about?' I asked. 'Presents for me?'

'No, I'm serious. I'm sorry, but I think that, fundamentally, you're not good enough for me. You don't care enough about other people, and you aren't motivated to do good.'

That stopped me in my tracks. 'What do you mean?'

'Well, like at that first place we lived in. You hated everyone.'

'They were awful.'

'No, they were just different from you.'

'Yes. They were awful.'

'Tova, for instance: she's really quite sweet. And Gayle – she's a nice girl, you just don't know her.'

'I don't want to know her.'

'You're always looking at people in the worst light.'

My defences began to give way. 'I suppose so . . .'

'And you're not kind to people in shops. Like that waitress the other day.'

'She was being stupid.'

'You think you're being assertive but you're just being mean. I dunno, Lins. It's, well . . . The people I'm meeting at work are happy to get along with each other, and they're not so judgemental, you know? They're just real people.'

Now I was on the attack. 'What the fuck's a "real person"?'

'You know what I'm talking about.'

'You said they were homogenous androids.'

'That's what I thought at first, but I don't want to approach life like that any more. I don't want to think the way you do . . . Don't cry, Lins. It's— There are so many things. Like with money. You always think people are out to rip you off. You don't want me to buy drinks and you always fuss at the tips I leave.'

'Jack, it's like you have this inferiority complex and have to prove you're not mean. You can't set foot in a bar without spending a hundred dollars, and we can't afford it.'

'Look, I know it's hard for you, with the way your family is, but I think you're—'

'What?'

'Morally inadequate.'

I was quiet for a bit. I had been brought up to expect the worst from life and the people in it. Jack might have been mad from time to time, but he was decent and friendly to people when he was sober. I didn't know what to do so I ran, sobbing, from the flat. It was exhilarating at first, but I soon felt the wind whipping through my rabbit-print pyjamas. And these were tough hills to negotiate in slippers.

When I got home, he rushed to embrace me. 'You know, Lins, in a way I think those things, but I'd gone and forgotten the fact that you're my lovely bunny. I'm sorry.'

We got the vodka from the kitchen, and made up lying down.

4: More drugs

'My daughter doesn't deserve a druggie!'
                                    Mum to Jack, 1995

Bit by bit, Jack's ancient habits were returning, and I nagged him round the clock. It was enough to drive a man to drink. Or cigarettes. Or weed. Or worse.

'Chief, please stop. Put it out. Please.'

'I'm going to stop. I'm not smoking that many, you know.'

'You're going to die.'

'I know. I'm going to stop.'

'When?'

He took a deep breath. 'Next week.'

'When you get cancer, I'm leaving you.'

'I know, Lins, it's just so hard, you know?'

'No, I don't know.'

'No, I know you don't know, but—'

'Please stop smoking, Jack. You've got to.'

'All right. Will you please shut up?'

'I'll shut up when you stop smoking.'

'I'm sick and tired of your nagging. You sound just like your mum.'

'I do not!'

Another old argument struck up yet again.

'Oh, go on, Lins.'

'Jack, I do not want to have anal sex.'

'Go on, you might like it.'

'Jack, I will not like it.'

'Please?'

'No. You tried before and it really hurt, remember? I made all that noise.'

'I'll be really gentle, Bun.'

'No.'

'Please?'

'No.'

I was at my wits' end with his smoking and bad moods. I'd tried nagging, pleading, reasoning, withholding, fighting and bitching. Anal sex was my last stronghold. 'Oh, all right then.' I sighed.

'Really, Bun?' His eyes lit up. 'All right, bend over, knickers down.'

'Not so fast,' I said, and laid out the deal. In return for every period of thirty-one documented, non-smoking days, Jack would get to fuck me up the arse once. We shook on it and he put his arm round me. He liked me again.

'You really will do it, Bunny? You'll really let me fuck you up the arse?'

'Yes.'

'Wow! That's amazing . . . I can't wait. I'll try with the ciggies, Lins, I'll really try.'

'Good.'

I'm not stupid. I knew his patterns: he'd strive, almost make the goal, and fail at the last minute. Then he'd strive again. I smiled at his childish enthusiasm, certain that this carrot would remain unchomped.

I didn't notice that I was losing control until we spent an evening with Jack's new workmates. We gathered towards sunset on glorious Baker Beach, and as the clouds rolled in round the bridge and the nudists called it a day, the gang set up a little bonfire and discreetly popped several bottles of champagne. An inky stain spread across the heavens. The sea broke heavily upon the shore, and I felt the sand damp beneath my thighs. Surrounded by strangers in silhouette, I hunkered down next to Jack. The darkness of the beach felt safe, but once we got to the gaudy Tex-Mex restaurant, my cover was blown. For the next five or six minutes, I was the centre of attention.

'I'm Jason,' grinned a Japanese-looking guy. 'So, I hear you play the accordion! That's cool! Hey, Stumford, your wife's cool!'

Another man approached. 'I'm Nate – Jack tells me you play the accordion! That's cool!'

A bleached-hair babe-type tottered over. This was Gayle. Finally we were face to face. 'Hi, Linda! It's great to meet you properly. I've heard so much about you! Wow, I love your hair! You play the accordion! Wow!' She gave the impression of being genuinely impressed. 'Jack is just so great!' she frothed. 'We all love him. He's so sweet and funny, just such a great guy. And he obviously adores you!'

'Thank you.' I checked out her gauzy pink top, clinging to a lacy, push-up underwired bra with a bow on it: 34B. She followed my gaze. 'What do you think of this, Linda? I was worried that maybe it's a bit see-through . . . you know?'

I assured her it was perfect, though I didn't say for what.

Then we were shown to our table, where I found myself adrift in a flood of inscrutable office banter. When the food arrived, it was as tasteless as the décor, but I was grateful for something to do. Jack was becoming too loud, and I leaned in for a quiet word. 'Chief,' I whispered, 'I think you've had enough to drink.'

The waiter swooped. 'Any more drinks?'

Jack raised his hand. 'Could I have a pint of Sierra, please?'

What was I to do?

The beer arrived before he'd finished his whisky and Jason laughed. 'Ooh! Stumford hasn't finished his whisky yet!' Desperate to stop Jack making a tit of himself, I tipped his whisky on to a vacant tortilla, pretending it was a joke. The crowd went silent. This was a blatant violation of Office Protocol: *Thou shalt not disrespect alcoholic beverages, especially when paid for by the boss, who is sitting at your table.*

'Lins!' cried Jack, aghast. 'What are you doing?'

The gang watched as the pool of whisky disappeared into the tortilla. It was as if I'd slain a kitten and the blood was draining from its neck. I think I heard the wall clock ticking above their heads.

When we got home, Jack was still livid. 'Why did you pour my drink away? It wasn't funny, it was just Wrong. It was Inappropriate.'

'You were drinking too much and mixing things and I knew you'd be ill.'

'I would not be ill! I don't get ill from drinking, hardly ever.'

'That's not true, you always get ill and it's a fucking pain in the arse.'

'You lying cow.'

'I'm not lying! Christ, Jack! So they all hate me now, right?'

'No, they just think you're weird, and that's a bad thing in their book. You made yourself look bad, Lins. I felt really embarrassed.'

'Sorry.'

They didn't ostracize him at work because of his control-freak wife. In fact, the next day, he came home smiling. 'Guess what Gayle said to me?'

'What?'

'"Oh, Mr Stumford, I'd definitely make a pass at you if you weren't married!" Can you believe it?'

'Yes. You're good-looking, and there's not much competition at the office.'

'Jason's good-looking.'

'He's short.'

'Not everyone thinks like you do. You should be more open-minded. Anyway, I thought it was sweet of Gayle to say that.'

'Sweet?'

'Yeah, I mean, she wasn't coming on to me, she just said she would if she could. She was paying me a compliment.'

'Jack! You were supposed to say, "Never mind the wife, let's get it on"!'

'You think?'

'Yes – you missed your big chance.' I wrapped my arms round him for a pre-dinner kiss, but he jolted his head back.

'Lins, could you do something about your nose hair? You really ought to trim it, you know. It's not very appealing.'

I went off to find the nail scissors.

The next day, the phone rang. It was 'Laura from Create! How *are* you? . . . Great. I have some exciting news. I have work for you! It's going to be a really cool project.'

'What is it?'

'It's writing a website for a really great company called Bathrooms Deluxe. They make toilets! Designer toilets. I immediately thought of you – you'd be perfect.'

'Great!'

'I'll send your stuff to the client and get back to you as soon as possible.'

My leaden mood lifted. This was so bad it was good, and I was happy to have some good news for Jack. 'Well done, Bun!' he said. 'Hey – let's have anal sex to celebrate.'

'No.'

The last stronghold down

Nine p.m., Friday, 21 September 2000. I had only a few hours left. Soon I would be twenty-eight. Jack and I met T&T in a womb-like underground bar called Café du Nord, and started downing vodkas.

As we surfaced for round three, the live act got under way and we started bobbing away at the back of the crowd.

After a good hour, T&T said their goodbyes. 'Stay for another drink!' cried Jack, putting down another twenty dollars and handing out the shots.

I leaned in. 'Chief, we don't have to buy everything.'

'Well, *they*'re not gonna, are they?'

'They don't want the drinks.'

'Lightweights!'

'Can we just slow down? We've already spent a hundred dollars.'

'Don't be such a tight-arse, Lins,' he snapped, and bought yet another round. T&T said they really had to go, so Jack finished their drinks too, but before I could get too annoyed, he picked me up and kissed me and spun me round.

A girl came out of the crowd and shouted through the noise: 'You two are, like, so in tune with each other! It's really cool.'

Dizzy with requited love, I popped to the loo, but when I got back my man was missing. I went to the bar: no Jack. Outside: no Jack. I couldn't see him in the crowd, either. Assuming he'd gone to the loo, I waited. And that was how I turned twenty-eight, standing outside a lavatory.

Just after midnight the show ended, and as I pulled on my coat, Jack came lurching out of the darkness towards me, blood running from his mouth. 'Bunny!' He gave me a big squeeze and spun me round so my feet came off the floor. I didn't feel safe.

'What happened, Chief?'

'They threw me out!'

'What? Why?'

The singer hadn't liked the grinning, yellow-shirted, giant pogo-dancer in the front row, and had asked Security to get rid of him. They'd dragged him out of the back of the club and he'd fought back, like he'd fought the policemen on top of the narrow-boat. He was laughing, so at least one of us had a good time. When we got home, he slapped my backside.

'One week, Bun!'

'You've managed a whole week without smoking?'

'Yup!'

'Seven days? In a row?'

'Yup! Just twenty-four to go and you know what happens . . .'

'Well, you keep at it, Chief.'

My plan seemed to be working – he had reduced his smoking considerably, but consistently failed to get anywhere near a month. I was congratulating myself when he spun me round: 'Let's see then, come on. Knickers down. Lovely. Hmm. Though . . . it's been trimmer, Bun, it's been trimmer.'

The next day was my real birthday, and we spent it going to things that were shut. We even got to the pedal-boats in the park just as they were closing for the night. Jack didn't get me a present or a card, but he did pay for an origami kit after I'd made a heavy hint: 'Will you buy me that origami kit for my birthday, please?' I had learned long ago that, anal sex aside, if I wanted something from Jack, I had to push. On my twenty-third birthday, I'd had to burst into tears before he bought me a copy of *Marie Claire* and an Aero. So many years had passed, and it seemed as though nothing had changed. As the sun set, we walked through the park arguing, then quarrelled our way through dinner. Fortunately, we had an event to attend after that – a burn on the vast, windswept plains of Ocean Beach, hosted by my one and only local contact:

Name: Mickie

Age: 29

Appearance: large nose, medium height

Philosophy: relax!

Occupation: socializing

Manner: casual, despite the suits
Liked:
- petite, curly-haired women
- most other types of women
- other people
- cocaine, speed, etc.
- giving cocaine, speed, etc. to other people
- singing, gently

I'd met him that summer at a wedding in Italy where he had tried to seduce every female, save the bride. 'Marriage in California doesn't count in Europe,' he'd breathed into my ear, then performed a heartfelt rendition of 'I Only Have Eyes For You' before diving into a bush with someone's little sister. Later they'd snuck back to the convent, where we were all staying, and had sex in her dorm.

I was glad he'd invited us to his beach burn. Dozens of golden fires crackled on the seemingly endless sands, so we didn't have to spend too long trekking in the cold. 'Linda!' beamed our host. 'Happy birthday!' He stuck out his hand to Jack. 'And you must be the Chief. Pleased to meet you.'

'Likewise.'

Mickie had a way with women, leaving all his relationships ajar, in case somebody else came along. This they did, at an astonishing rate. Perhaps not so astonishing – he had a generous heart and the trust fund to prove it. To get hold of the money, he'd had to appease his grandpa by studying engineering. The old man survived to see him graduate, so he'd wasted another three years getting a master's – it was either that or actually work as an engineer. Finally, the Grim Reaper come to pay his respects, saving the grandson from a lifetime of gainful employment, but 168 hours' free time a week proved a mixed blessing. His fun-packed schedule looked something like this:

- 8 p.m. to 3 a.m. socializing and/or having sex
- 3 a.m. to noon   sleeping and/or having sex
- noon to 8 p.m.   recovering, worrying and planning

It was the noon to eight p.m. slot that caused all the trouble. He'd spend the long daylight hours organizing his social life, fretting about his undone errands, helping his friends and taking random classes in Italian, upholstery, singing, yoga and piano. He even took accordion lessons from me for a while. Slumped over the unwieldy instrument, he'd grope blindly for the buttons as I folded my arms and sighed. 'You haven't practised, have you?'

He'd turn his puppy-dog eyes on me. 'I do try, you know, Linda.'

'No, you don't.'

'I do – I slept with the accordion last night!'

'You what?'

'I put it on the bed, on top of me. I thought if it was there when I woke up, I might decide to stay in bed and practise.'

'But you didn't.'

'No.'

'So what are you going to do?'

'I've got a great idea.'

'Yes?'

'Let's go to lunch. My treat.'

Over roasted tofu spare ribs with lemongrass, he told me of his struggles. 'I have a perfect life, Linda. It's a shame I don't enjoy it more.'

Initially, I put his lethargy down to my own shortcomings as an entertainer, but then I learned the truth. 'By Thursday I've got all these things to get done, so I take a bit of crank, and then I can get my bills and the household chores done. Then I get cranked up again on Friday and Saturday to have fun, and then I have to on Sunday too.'

'Why?'

'Because otherwise I can't get out of bed.'

Chasing women took so much out of him, there wasn't much left for the main event. 'I take them home,' he confided, 'and then I disappoint them.'

I thought of all those women, thwarted on the brink of ecstasy. 'I know it's tedious,' I said tediously, 'but you really should try exercise, Mickie. It's like magic fuel that lasts all day, unless you're depressed.'

He replied, graven-faced, 'It's not that simple. I've got a heart condition.'

I was aghast. 'And you take all that speed?'

'Crank, honey, crank. Look, it's either drugs or exercise, but not both. My doctor said the combination would kill me! I've made my choice.'

Jack and I joined the group round the fire, a cheery flicker against the black depths of sea and sky. I managed to cobble together some chat with those next to me, but it was too much for Jack, who sat there feeling inept and downing vodka. When he started throwing beer bottles into the blaze, I realized I'd neglected him too long. By the time he'd reached the 0.5-litre mark, he was leaping about perilously close to the flames and people were complaining.

'Please, Jack,' I begged, 'please don't drink any more.'

'Fuck you!'

'Please.'

'Fuck you, bitch!' He stalked off towards the Pacific Ocean. 'I'm going to drown myself!' The currents were so powerful that he had every chance of success, so I grabbed a flashlight and kept it trained on him. 'Jack!' I screeched. 'Come back!'

After twenty minutes, he emerged from the waves. He rolled ecstatically in the sand, then crawled over and gave me a big, wet, sandy cuddle. I struggled free and sat next to Mickie, who suddenly rolled off to the right – he'd seen Jack coming from above. It was a heavy landing.

Shortly afterwards, Mickie took me to one side. 'Listen, Linda. I think it might be time to take Jack home.'

'Yeah . . .'

'I'm about ready to go. Do you two want a ride? You live a-ways away, don't you?'

I apologized, but Jack had run back into the ocean. 'Come on, Chief,' I yelled. 'Get out of the water. We're leaving.'

'Hah!'

'Come on, get out. We've got a lift.'

'Hah! Bunny!' He emerged once again, dripping. 'Had to get my jeans clean!'

His efforts had been in vain, as he fell over eight times (yes, I counted) on the way to the jeep, and was soon covered with sand again. At last, he was strapped into the car, holding his head in his hands. He groaned the whole way home and I feared the worst, given the poor suspension and the hills. Somehow we made it without any vomiting, and I got Jack out of the car. 'So sorry,' I said, shutting Mickie's door and waving goodbye. I turned to find Jack spreadeagled on the pavement. Somehow his shoes had come off. 'Chief, stand up. You've got to go into the house.'

'M'Bun! Hah! Not going!'

'Chief, stand up. Get up, please. Chief, you've got to get up. Jack. Get up.'

I tugged at his leg and, inch by inch, persuaded him to crawl up the steps. It took about fifteen minutes. As he was covered with sand, I told him to get into the shower, but he kept slipping and telling me to fuck off. Every time he said it, I cried. And finally, he puked all over the loo. Cleaning it off the bowl was a fitting end to the night.

He regained consciousness the next afternoon. I told him what had happened, but he wasn't having it. 'You're so full of shit, Lins. So full of shit.'

73

'So what's that?' I pointed at the crusted clothing, strewn in a line towards the bathroom.

He followed my finger with his eyes, and groaned softly. 'Oh, shit.'

The phone rang. 'Hello, darling, it's Mum. I don't have anything special to say, just wanted to speak to my wee girl. Now, are you warm enough? Do you need a blanket?'

'Mum, I'm in California.'

'I know, darling, but it's a strange country. Your mother loves you very much.'

'I know. I love you too, Mum.'

Somehow, when I really needed a little support, it turned up. And, right on cue, the phone rang again. It was Laura from Create! I was glad to hear from her, because I was anxious to get on with that loo job.

'Hi, Linda!' she trilled. 'How *are* you? Listen, I'm afraid I have bad news. Bathrooms Deluxe decided you weren't the person for them.'

'Oh.' I was gutted. I'd been counting on this. 'Did they say why?'

'They said you weren't wacky enough. I know it doesn't really tally with your abilities, but all they had to go on was your website samples, and they're pretty straight. You know, you need to put up something that really demonstrates your capabilities. I'm so sorry.'

I put the phone down. After the first wave of tears, I continued crying because I was crying about being rejected by a lavatory manufacturer.

Meanwhile Jack's expenses were increasing. He was starting to buy weed. 'You can't expect me just to sponge off the guys at work all the time; I have to contribute.'

Come the weekend, we'd often wander to Haight Street, me attracted by the thrift stores, Jack by the drug-dealers. I'd be trying on a frilly shirt I didn't need, only to find myself abandoned with a kiss and a whisper: 'Back in ten minutes, Bun.' For a man raised on a chicken farm, these assignations had a 'keepin' it real' appeal, but for me it was a big drag. I found getting stoned equally tiresome, but he got much more out of it:

- slurred speech
- increased ability to bore others
- red-rimmed eyes
- short-term memory loss (recurring)
- increased appetite for impenetrable poetry
- marked hostility

'Bollocks!' he insisted, but couldn't deny my ability to spot it immediately, even over the phone. Still, he found excuses to keep buying the stuff.

'Ooow.'

I ignored Jack and kept on walking.

'Ooow,' he repeated, a little more insistently.

This happened every time he'd gone without cigarettes for more than a day.

'Ow. Oooooh. Oooow. *Ouch*!'

He claimed withdrawal symptoms, similar to bad flu. I was suffering too, as he had taken to giving up smoking on Friday nights, then spending the whole weekend moaning. Come Monday morning, he was overcome with work pressures and started smoking again.

'It's too much without it, Lins. Too damned much.'

I was unsympathetic. 'Mmm.'

'Ow. Ooooow. Aarrrrgh.'

I gave in. 'What's wrong, Chief?'

'Oow, you don't know how bad it is, Lins. It's just torture. All my nerves are tingling. I need to get some weed, just today. I know I said I'd stop buying it, but it'll really help.'

'Please don't, Jack. Apart from anything, we can't afford it. There's almost nothing left in my bank account.' This was true. I'd been offered nothing further by Create!, and had contacted more than a

75

hundred agencies without any productive responses. I was writing a lot of songs and getting better at the accordion, but that wasn't in the Plan.

'OK,' he replied. 'You're right.'

But three paces on he kissed my head and skipped off, saying, 'Meet you in that café at ten past!' Within yards he'd found a dealer, who led him in an elaborate dance while I sat self-consciously in the café, trying to look as if I had friends. Suddenly there was Jack. An early reprieve!

'Can I have some cash, Lins? He'll only sell a hundred and twenty dollars' worth.'

My smile gone, I went to the cashpoint and sourly handed him the notes. 'Thanks, Bun!' He kissed me and sped off, returning with a jaunty swagger and going straight to the loo to check out the goods. He emerged with a visible stoop. 'I can't believe it.'

'What?'

'I've been done. The bastard! This is just herbs.'

'Jack,' I said calmly, 'you are a fucking idiot.'

'I know. I can't buy this shit again. That's it, Lins. Never again.'

'Mmm.'

I stirred my coffee dregs with a plastic fork.

Eventually the dreaded day arrived: he jumped into bed and tapped me on the shoulder. 'OK, roll over.'

'Huh?'

'Thirty-one days. I've done it. You owe me.'

'Really?'

'Yup.'

'When did you last have a fag?'

'On the eighth.'

'How do you know?'

'I put it in my diary.'

'I'll make you banoffee pie every night this week.'

'Roll over.'

'With three tins of condensed milk.'

'No can do.'

I tried whimpering. 'Please, Chief, I don't want to.'

'But you promised me.'

'I know, but . . .'

'So it was all for nothing? I'll start fucking chain-smoking again, then. Jesus Christ, Linda. I might have known. I'm off to the shop.' He leaped out of bed.

I held on to his arm and pulled him back. 'No, it's fine. I'm sorry. Come on.'

His frown flipped up into a smile. 'Really? You'll do it?'

'Yes.'

'I don't want to hurt you.'

'It's OK.'

'Are you sure?'

For the thousandth time I pictured him in a white hospital gown, bald and skeletal with oxygen tubes in his nose.

'Yes.'

'Great!' he said. 'I'll get the Vaseline.'

No Butts

There's very little that I won't do in bed,
Behind a pillar or in a garden shed,
But there is one little thing I really cannot bear,
And that's being taken up the derrière.

I am as sick and as twisted as they come,
Except in matters pertaining to my bum,
So while I do hate to be a tedious boudoir bore,
Please don't come knocking on my back door.

If you don't wish to inspire my disdain,
Then I must ask you to use the other lane
Because it feels like I'm defecating, only then
It all decides to come back in again.

I don't bend over to make you love me more
For if I do so, I know just what's in store.
So when you say that you love me, darling, please do try
To make sure you can look me in the eye.

Just as I'd expected, it hurt like buggery.

5: The Trouble with Mum and Dad

'Don't have children, my darling, they ruin your life.'
                                                    Mum

My parents were coming to stay for five weeks. It was during this interminable episode that Jack decided he wanted to have sex with other people and tell me all about it.

The parental visit was my idea. We'd spent the past three Christmases with Jack's relatives so mine were long overdue their turn. However, Christmas at their house was a treeless, giftless, joyless misery. It hadn't always been like that – I remember waking up to find my bed covered with gifts, but in 1978, Mum had complained that Dad never gave her anything, and he subsequently presented her with a doorbell. The next year she got a dustbin. 'And your mother says I never give her anything!' After that, our presents were steadily downgraded to A4 refill pads, multipacks of socks, and by 1986 Mum had given up completely.

I invited them to join us in the States, then found out that flight prices were sky high for five whole weeks. My parents lived and breathed bargains: it was out of the question for them to travel at peak rate, but I didn't want to disappoint them. Nor did I want to go home.

'Five weeks?' gasped Mum. 'Don't you think that's too long, darling? We don't want to outstay our welcome.'

I took a deep breath. I had to mean this. 'No, don't be silly. It'll be lovely to see you for a proper amount of time.' I vowed to exonerate myself from past lapses. As I explained to Jack, this time it would be good.

'Five *weeks*? Lins, what the hell were you thinking?'

Why this negative attitude? you may ask. Well, back in England, this would have been a typical family scene:

'MUM! JUST STOP FUCKING NAGGING! I'm going to get the right milk. Stay there! Sit down! Dad's not put his thumb in it. It's fine.'

'He sticks his filthy fingers in the spout! He's a disgusting man!'

'I'll wash the damned jug, all right? I'll bring through the right milk.'

'He's always giving me the full fat, and I can't take it – IT MAKES ME SICK!'

'I've got your milk here. That's your little jug, isn't it?'

'And then he puts the carton down on the table! I hate it! We're not gypsies! I like milk in a JUG!'

'Do you want a tea biscuit, Mum?'

'Yes, please, darling. TELL YOUR FATHER HE'S AN IDIOT!'

Dad took the carton of full-fat milk through and plonked it in front of her. 'Calm down, woman,' he said. 'Be at peace.'

After the ritual ordeal of tea-time, I stood in their hermetically sealed kitchen, looking at the back garden. Dad had gone out to mow the lawn. He was a thin man who said little and spent less, and didn't seem to feel much either, though this was partly a matter of style. 'Over the years with your mother,' he liked to say, 'I've developed marital deafness.' During her attacks, he would make an auto-response every few minutes: 'All right, Davina. You've had your say.' It drove her crazy – she couldn't even make him hate her. She tended to step up the marital abuse when I was around: at least then she knew that *someone* was listening.

I went outside to ask him what he wanted for dinner.

'Eh . . . I think,' he muttered, flicking clumps of grass off the blade, 'it's um, we'll, er, go out.'

'Go *out*?' What was going on? We didn't just *go out*.

'It's, eh, your mother . . . anniversary.'

'Oh, it's your wedding anniversary? That's nice.'

'Aye, Black Saturday. Forty years ago today. I can hardly believe it.'

'I didn't realize it was today.'

'Well, we don't normally do anything, but I suppose forty's quite a significant one.'

'So where are we going?' As if I had to ask.

'Um.' He paused, pretending to think. 'Captain Fiddlesticks suit you?'

It wasn't really a question. Captain Fiddlesticks was the tarted-up chain-pub down the road. It had the usual large-portion/low-price/ no-taste combo, but distinguished itself from regular pubs by having plastic-coated menus instead of a blackboard. I knew that Mum wouldn't be pleased. 'I hate eating in pubs! Your father always drags me into a pub when we're out, and the smell of the grease makes me sick. They always give you huge portions, and everything's oily and tough. I can't eat it! Just because he wants a beer – he's got to have his damned beer. If I find a nice little café, he won't go in. He's such a selfish man, Linda, but that's the Robertsons, through and through.' Though I look like my dad would after a sex change, it never seemed to strike her that I was half Robertson. I left Dad to his clippings and went back into the house.

Mum was upstairs, sorting through the rainbow snakepit of her zip bucket. She looked up at me and smiled. 'Hello, darling. I've got so many of these things. It's such a mess. One of these days I'll get myself organized.'

'Er,' I began, 'Dad says we're going out for dinner.'

Her smile fell, and she let go of a bouquet of orangy zips, which slithered into her lap. 'Yes,' she said. 'It's our anniversary.'

'That's nice.'

'I was hoping he'd forgotten.'

'I think it's quite sweet that he remembered.'

'I can't believe it, Linda. I suppose it is nice of him.'

'Um, he wants us to go to Captain Fiddlesticks.' I braced myself for the backlash, but she was strangely resigned to her fate.

'I suppose we'd better go. After all, when will he offer to take us out again?'

'I could try and get him to take us somewhere a bit better.'

'No, darling, he won't do it. Just go along with it. Please your father for me.'

She was being so amenable! Perhaps this would be all right, after all.

By six p.m. we were sitting at a table for ten in a deserted eating section. Around us, the air was alive with the sound of shitty music; I was trapped in a tin can with some angry wasps. Still, at least we looked good: Mum had painted on some lips (the originals having virtually disappeared), and pulled on a fluffy jacket with glittery bits, I had found a dress and I'd forced Dad to change out of his gardening gear. 'I can't stand the smell of the oil here!' Mum barked. 'Makes me feel sick!'

Politely ignoring her plight, we ordered drinks and studied the giant shiny menus, ablaze with full-colour meat pornography. Everything was hot, moist and anxious to please – chops glistened, sausages gleamed, steaks oozed blood, and a pink swathe of salmon beckoned from its tepid bath of white sauce. When I looked up from this carnage, Dad belched luxuriantly. 'Something I like about this place,' he said, pushing his specs back with a muddy finger, 'there isn't that dreadful *pop music* playing in the background.'

I inserted the blade of my knife between my fork tines and scraped it up and down. In a quiet voice, I told him that there was indeed dreadful *pop music* playing in the background.

'You're talking rubbish, Linda!' He craned his head to the left, then to the right, wearing a puzzled expression. 'I can't hear anything.'

Wearily, Mum chimed in: 'They're playing music, Alec.'

'You think so?' He shrugged his shoulders. 'Well, you might be right . . .'

These days, Mum could only eat bird-size portions. She asked for a Kiddie Fun Meal.

'I'm sorry, madam,' said the waiter, 'but you're too old.'

She couldn't argue with that so she had a starter instead. Dad and I chose a main course and our frozen, microwaved, deep-fried meals arrived promptly on heavy white plates.

Mum's starter proved too much for her. 'I can't stand seeing a full plate these days,' she said, scraping a few bites on to a saucer and pushing the rest away. 'Take that away, could you, Linda?' I hid her excess food behind the sugar bowl.

'Food not suit you, Bug?' asked Dad, as though he'd never seen her act like this before.

'Alec,' she said tersely, 'I have a lot of problems eating, in case you haven't noticed.'

'Can't eat a lot? You, with your big fat bottom?'

This felt like a script for a nightmarish play. But no one changed the lights or gave us a prompt. 'Dad,' I said flatly, 'Mum's bottom is the same size as yours these days.'

'Is it? Great big bottom like that?'

He was using his classic autopilot responses, doing his best to keep things upbeat, forging blindly ahead with the old jokes, but my poor, skinny mum wasn't having it. 'Your father doesn't notice anything,' she informed me quietly, then turned to him, unleashing a sudden tempest. 'Alec, I am NOT FAT! In case you haven't noticed, I'm WASTING AWAY! The flesh is hanging off my backside, or haven't you noticed?'

'You just need ironing, Bug!'

'Bastard!'

'All right, Davina, calm down and eat your food.'

He ran his index finger down her nose, an act of strangulated affection that always sent her into a rage. She brushed him off, picked up one of the giant menus from another table and set it up round her plate. 'I can't stand to see him,' she hissed, from behind her flimsy barricade, her face replaced with an image of a towering chocolate sundae.

I swallowed a piece of rubbery salmon. 'Mmm,' I enthused, 'my fish is really nice. How's yours, Dad?'

'Oh, very good, yes. I can't get a decent meal at home, you understand. I'm trying to teach your mother to cook, but she's a slow learner.'

A thin voice rose from behind the plastic-coated screen. 'Always the same phrases, Alec. Can't you say something new? We're sick of them. Sick and tired.'

He raised his glass. 'Cheers, one and all.'

'Cheers.' I downed my whisky and Mum glumly stirred her tea. Her liver was screwed up so she couldn't touch alcohol.

'Well,' said Dad, pressing on gamely, 'we've been married forty years, so, happy anniversary. The sixth of June 1960 . . .'

A sad voice rose from behind the menu. 'Aye, happy anniversary.'

'Forty years.'

'Thank God it's over.'

'Quite,' agreed Dad. 'Well, Davina, at least there won't be another forty years.'

She spat a tough piece of chicken on to her plate. 'You can bet your life on that.'

They had married because they liked each other, but they'd never admit it. Mum would sometimes tell me about the past when we were alone together.

'We used to chase each other round the bedroom. Can you believe it?'

Looking at the black-and-white pictures, I can. There are my parents, fresh-looking, with thick, wavy hair and unstrained smiles. My dad doesn't have so many chins – he looks vulnerable and fun, always about to step lightly out of the frame. Mum has a great tartan wardrobe and stands her ground.

They met at a dance near Glasgow. Dad drove her home, and said he'd like to see her again but couldn't because he was moving the next day. She thought he was blowing her off, but it was true – from seventeen to twenty-nine, he moved jobs every three weeks, stepping into the breach every time a Scottish tax inspector went on holiday. This set-up kept him single but paid so well that he could afford a wife and most of a house by the time he was thirty.

Davina recognized him when he came back to the dance hall two years later. 'Remember me?' she asked.

'I can't say I do . . .'

(I asked him about this, and he said, 'Oh, Linda, I was meeting so many people, all the time, I couldn't possibly keep up. I stopped trying to remember.'

'When was that, then?'

He put his fingers on his chin and furrowed his brow. 'Oh, about 1957 or thereabouts.')

Not to worry: she made a brand-new impression that night, her strong body wrapped prettily in a dress cut expertly from old curtains. This was a woman with boundless energy and thrifty domestic talents, and here was a man with a good job and a sense of humour, which he needed on the dance-floor. 'Oh,' chuckled Mum, remembering that night, 'your father was a terrible dancer.' But something about his awkwardness had touched her. Unassuming yet resolute, he had proved to be the only man with the resilience to thwart her Guardian, Aunt Mary.

Four feet ten on a good day, this unfortunate lady had been doomed to spinsterhood by rickets, a sharp tongue, and the First World War. It was easier, however, to blame Davina, her sister's child, whose father had never been around and whom Aunt Mary had ended up mothering. They had lived together in the family home until Davina was three, when the sister married an Englishman and moved to London, leaving her daughter behind. She had no mum, no dad, and no money, but made the most of her array of talents, from playing hockey, tennis, squash and the piano to baking, gardening, decorating and sewing; she had learned that to be loved she had to be useful. Her burdens as a child had included the shopping, the cooking, the cleaning, the gardening and the decorating. Each night after school she'd brought in the coal to light the fire in an empty house, and vowed that her children would come home to a warm kitchen with a mother in it who had done all the chores. She whacked balls over nets and fields and, although she lived in a council house with no literature beyond the phone book, she managed to get to college, become a PE teacher and not get pregnant, or anywhere near it. Her goal was to create a happy family and, as usual, she was playing to win.

Alec represented the security of the home-owning class. The son of two snobbish teachers who never went near him, he was immune to aesthetics, unathletic, clever and possessed of total integrity. He would never buy her flowers, and he would never let her down. They married in 1960, and by 1970 they had a little house in Dundee, and a seven-year-old son. 'When my children were young,' Mum used to say, 'was the happiest time in my life.'

One freezing January night they went off to a neighbour's party, and Aunt Mary came over to babysit. When they returned, Aunt Mary said the boy had been complaining of a headache. Mum went to check on him and told my father she was going to call the doctor. Dad hated to be a pest. 'Davina, you mustn't go bothering folk . . .'

She persisted, and about forty minutes later a doctor arrived. He pressed the boy's skin with a stethoscope. It left purple marks that didn't fade, and he knew it was meningitis. He administered the drugs, late as it was, and Mum spent the night in a bedside vigil, leaning over her son's little body. The bruises spread further and further over his white skin, like inky stains on blotting-paper. He died in the pallid light of dawn.

Thirty years later, Mum couldn't say his name without crying. Sometimes when I kept her up, talking late at night, she'd get suddenly furious: 'Ach, Linda, leave me alone! You're so like your brother – he used to talk at me, on and on, he wouldn't stop! I can't stand it!' She'd be in tears.

Dad always shook his head, and said the same thing: 'He was running around the night before, a perfectly healthy wee lad, and he was dead before the next morning. Yes, we could have done very nicely without that. Very nicely indeed.' The words he used might have described a minor irritation, like a traffic jam, but he would always look away into the corner of whichever room we were sitting in.

The local paper covered the story, and a big crowd attended the funeral. The questions my parents asked themselves for the rest of their lives – why had they gone out? What if they'd got to him sooner? – were whispered by guests sipping cups of strong tea. After the ceremony, a woman in the crowd came up and told my dad that 'If that was my son, he wouldn't be under the ground now.'

Dad just looked at her, and never told Mum about it: 'Oh, it would only have made her feel worse.'

After all the guests had gone home and the flowers had faded, there they were, still alive. Mum carried on looking after the house, while Dad carried on going to work, inspecting taxes by day and crying himself to sleep at night. This went on for six months; Mum said he made the bed shake so hard, she couldn't get a wink of sleep. That's how I know he must love me too.

Mum gave up on God: 'I don't care if he exists or not. If that's the kind of thing he does to me, I don't want to know him.' They stopped taking family photos. The doctor said the only way she would recover would be to have another baby – I was prescribed. Thus, thirty months and two miscarriages later, I arrived. My nickname was Precious Pearl. My role was simple: to make the world good again.

To this end, I was given every assistance. Mum used to make tapes of herself reading bedtime stories for when she had to go out, and told the babysitter to play them to me. Then she'd call the sitter several times during the evening: 'Everything all right?' As soon as I was able to toddle into danger, I was fitted with reins. My internal chemistry aligned itself with the atmosphere of fear and kitted me out with a hyperactive immune system that leaped to my defence, staging violent allergic reactions against such harmless enemies as eggs, dogs and summer weather. Each August it glued the backs of my legs together with weeping eczema, and I'd screech while Mum eased open the sticky hinges and rubbed vicious steroid cream into the blazing mess. I still have the scars. The rash crept over my face, and I'd try to hide my crusted lips by curling them back over my teeth. At nursery school, I got my first social scar when I asked three girls if I could play with them. 'No!' cried the leader. 'Go away, Crocodile Skin!'

I had become allergic to eggs aged four, exploding dramatically at the slightest exposure – mouth swelling, vomit spraying, tears flowing. When I was six, we discovered my allergy to dogs when visiting Auntie Pat and her eight Scottish terriers. They were every-where, unstoppable, like giant fleas, their nasty spittly tongues leaving my face, neck and hands covered in red weals. Asthma kicked in at nine, and I wheezed my way through many a long night, often awakening from nightmares about drowning to struggle for breath. Few germs made it through my overwrought safety shield, but if they did, and I became genuinely ill, I was given a little bell and twenty-four-hour room service. Mum didn't let me leave the cul-de-sac alone until I was ten. It was a concrete jungle out there. 'If anything happens to you, Mummy will die. I'll just die. Or I'll kill myself.'

The constant threat of death makes it hard to be adventurous, and it certainly made school swimming classes more challenging as I couldn't put my head under water for fear of drowning. I remember cowering on the three-metre platform as my classmates bobbed below me, calling in unison: 'Jump! Jump! Jump!' They didn't understand that things were different for me: I could actually die.

In 1980, my invincible mother started to complain of a variety of minor health problems, apparently unconnected. The doctor said she was a hypochondriac and Dad agreed wholeheartedly, as he preferred not to worry. Three years later, we left the concrete hem of Luton for the duckponds of the south, and our new doctor referred Mum to a specialist. To her apparent relief, it turned out that something was seriously wrong. 'You see?' she would cry triumphantly. 'I'm not crazy! I'm not a hypochondriac!'

And Dad would reply, 'These things are all in the mind!'

She was diagnosed with CREST syndrome, a rare wasting disease comprising five items, each of which causes about five symptoms, any of which can turn your life to shit and some of which can kill you. The main thrust of it is that all your tissues get replaced with scar tissue, stiff and inflexible. The more it affects your skin, the uglier you look. The more it affects your heart and lungs, the faster you die. Mum's affected her liver mainly, which screwed up every system in her body and put her in a permanently foul temper. Through research in the local library, she learned that she had about seven years to live, which she kept to herself until way past the deadline. Dad still trusted the old doctor, and joked about Mum's hypochondria, so she was forced to turn to me: 'There's no light at the end of the tunnel, Linda . . . I wish I was well enough to leave him . . . Your father's a cruel bastard . . . I should never have married him . . . I should have divorced him years ago . . . If only I could live alone . . . I can't carry on like this . . .' an endless mantra of domestic despair. It was safer to complain about a benign husband than a malevolent disease.

In forty-seven years as a tax inspector, my father didn't have one day off sick. After an appendix operation in 1953, he was fine until he had an epileptic fit in 2002 (which, I delighted in telling him, was 'all in the mind'). He even had his teeth. It wasn't fair. When they'd married, she'd weighed more than him, with all that muscle, and could beat him in every sport. Now she watched as he strode ahead then and waited impatiently on a bench as she wheezed towards him. The moment she caught up, he'd move on. He booked them into a cheap hotel at the top of a hill, and protested when she caught a cab home three times a day. He constantly turned off the central heating, although her extremities were blue. He bought a big new car with a gear lever, instead of an automatic, even though arthritis made it painful for her to drive it. He dropped her off for her appointments at the hospital, although she wanted him to wait with her. What was she making such a fuss about? 'It's all in the mind, Bug!'

I thought he was being selfish, but there was more to it. Unable to bear the thought of another death in the family, he had spent over twenty years pretending his wife was doing fine, while she became more embittered with each year that passed. She and I were beyond close; we were symbiotic. We were each other's best friend and confidante – I shared her bee-like attraction to bright clothes and flowers, and knew why crappy tapes of violin concertos made her exclaim with glee while she was doing her ironing. Once she knew she was dying, she held on to me extra tight. I loved and needed my mum, but I was tired of having an enmeshed soul and a shared brain with someone who believed the worst would happen, and had the experience to prove it. I'd breathed this sadness my whole life long; it was as familiar and imperceptible as my own heartbeat.

Jack's protests came too late. I'd found cheap tickets online and Dad was chuffed. 'Per mile,' he informed me, 'that's seventeen times cheaper than the bus to Winchester.' Up in the attic, Mum's preparations had already begun:

Dear Linda

*Your dad is raving at me to go out (for it's sunny and bright)
so I'll get this ready for the post and go with him and perhaps
get a nasty pub lunch. Please take care of yourself and phone
me when you have a spare few minutes. I love you and hope
that your friends are interesting you and treating you well,
and that you and Jack are happy in your sunny home. Let
me know if you need us to bring anything – we have lots of
blankets.*

Lots of love, Mum XXXXX

I smiled, thinking of their incessant delivery service. Our relationship had come to revolve around objects small, medium and large,
requested, sent, enquired after, acknowledged and forgotten. When
we moved into our first place in London, they'd brought a three-
month supply of loo paper; traipsing over by tube, they'd brought
eighteen luxury toilet rolls and some plants for the garden on a
shopping trolley. And they loved to bring us furniture, insisting
there was 'plenty more in the attic'. How true that was. The last
haul consisted of three optimistic tea-towels, one promoting the
national dress of Alsace, one advertising the sun-drenched beaches
of the south coast, the last festooned with Christmas stockings.
They were wrapped round a pair of outsize beige socks for Jack,
which had cost more than Mum or Dad would spend on a pair of
shoes, and two pairs of gloves for me from the Cancer Research
shop. All this arrived in a triple layer of Sellotaped bubble-
wrap – a type of burglar-proof, gas-impermeable seal that had
once caused a Richmond vicar to swear and reach for his carving
knife (he was letting me sleep on his dining-room floor and Mum
said thanks by sending him some new tea-towels). In addition to
this, there was a constant trickle of notes, newspaper cuttings and
postcards:

Post-modern Post

'Darling, I must run to catch the post, love Mum'
Your letter ends.
'Hope you're having fun, now I must get my ironing done'
Is all you send.

Oh, your writing is post-modern, totally self-referential,
It says nothing but you love me, the content is quite incidential.

'Did you get my note? I can't remember what I wrote!'
Your letter ends.
'Just a note to say hello, and now I've got to go!'
Is all you send.

Oh, your writing is post-modern, totally self-referential,
It says nothing but you love me, which makes me feel quite sentimential!

You tell my friend to tell me there's a message on my phone.
This says you've emailed me:
'Darling, have I logged on? I think I've done something wrong!'
Is all there is to see.

Oh, your writing is post-modern, totally self-referential,
It says nothing but you love me, to say more would be quite detrimential!

The day of their arrival was marked by a freak rainstorm. 'At least they'll feel at home.' I sighed, my eyes on the leaden skies. Mum was too tired to smile. She had vomit on her trousers and they'd rolled her off the plane in a wheelchair. 'And you know, darling,' she gasped, in a faint monotone, 'that was marvellous ... We didn't have to wait in that ... big queue ... We just went straight through ...'

I put her to bed. 'Let's have those trousers off. I'll get you a hottie. Do you want a cup of tea?'

'Yes, darling, three sugars ... Remember to stir it ... never enough sugar ... Your father ... oh, Linda, he's such a bastard! He had me ... oh, that's lovely ...'

Be it in a teacup, a rubber bottle or a bathtub, she could always be silenced with hot water.

Later that day, we sat before an easy-to-eat dinner of chicken, mashed potato and asparagus. 'What's this?' asked Dad, holding aloft a green spear.

'Asparagus,' I said.

'As-*par*-a-gus?'

'It's optional.'

'Glad to hear it. Well, I'll say grace. For God's sake, begin!'

Mum took a sad nibble. She got no pleasure from her food any more. 'This is lovely, darling, thank you so much.'

'Not bad,' chimed in Dad. 'You're learning! I don't get to eat good food at home, you understand.'

'Oh, Alec, when will you change the record?'

'Be at peace, woman.'

She turned to me. 'Where's Jack got to, darling?'

He was writing a poem about the ineffable nature of time. When I called his name, he came into the kitchen, stopped in his tracks, and stared at his plate. 'Is that fried?' he demanded.

'It's sautéed.'

'I said I didn't want anything fried for a while.'

'Then you said you really liked fried chicken.'

'No, I didn't.'

'Yes, you did.' He'd fried his own memory with all that weed.

'You just make these things up. Well, I'll get something later.' He stomped back towards the door.

Dad looked up, incredulous. 'Are you no' eating, Jack?'

'I'm afraid it's not something I like, Alec.'

93

'It'th lovely chicken, Jack,' mumbled Mum, grinding painfully away with her false teeth. 'Try it, love. Linda'th done a lovely job.'

He sat down and sullenly ate his mashed potato.

Despite this, week one was enjoyable. I'd actually found it a comfort to have Mum and Dad in this foreign land, and there'd been so many new things to see, Mum and I strolling slowly around the botanical gardens while Dad checked out the farmers' markets. But now we had reached week two. Each morning, Mum sat in the kitchen, resonating despair, transfixed by her sodden cornflakes. A grey dressing-gown hung from her pathetic frame. As she'd lost weight over the last few years, her brilliant wardrobe had been replaced with smaller, greyer garments. 'Mum,' I asked, 'what's the matter? Are you OK?'

She didn't answer. Dad, oblivious to the emotional drama, launched into one of his signature tunes.

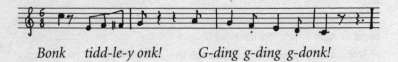

Bonk   tidd-le-y onk!   G-ding g-ding g-donk!

'It's just that you seem very unhappy, Mum. Is it something I can do anything about?'

'No, darling, it's nothing,' she snivelled. 'It's not you, it's just' – she glared at Dad – 'what it's always been!'

He glanced up from his crossword and looked at her over his specs. 'I'm no' doing anything! Be at peace, woman.' He ran his index finger down her nose and she burst into tears, or what would have been tears if her eyes hadn't dried up. She had artificial tears in a spray can. I offered her more tea.

'Yes, please, darling.' She sniffed. 'Three sugars, please, and make sure you stir it. It's never sweet enough.'

Eating out in San Francisco with my parents was extremely diffi-cult as they sought food that was indigenous to Scotland, cheap, bland and served by people whose first language was English. This disqualified crêpes (F), falafel (F), kebabs (F), pizza (F), pasta (F), noodles (F, S), burritos (F, S, D of A), curry (F, S), salad (D of A), sushi (W), tapas (F), and burgers (TBB).[9] In addition, they both LOATHED mushrooms, and Mum had to avoid anything fatty (the liver problems), bitty (got stuck under her dentures), or crunchier than mashed potato (mouth ulcers). Then there was the size issue. American portions were an outrage. 'Oh, Christ,' grunted Dad, eyeing his Basic Breakfast. 'That's bloody ridiculous.'

Meanwhile Mum was dismayed by her pancake stack. 'Oh, no. How am I supposed to get through all this? No wonder Americans are so fat.'

'Think about it,' I said, gritting my teeth, 'if someone was running a restaurant and served portions to suit the two of you, they wouldn't last very long, would they? They have to provide enough food for normal people.'

They agreed, grudgingly, but it hurt them to waste food, partly because they'd grown up with ration books, and partly because – theoretically – they could have paid half as much. I began counting the days until the Christmas trip – I'd booked up a load of treats, and was sure that things would be better once we were on the move.

The tale of the Christmas trip

'I hate Christmas.'
Mum

From the moment we set off it was all downhill, except for the road, which was partially uphill. I'd rented a smooth, inscrutable

9 F = Foreign, S = Spicy, D of A = Danger of Avocado, W = Weird, TBB = Too Bloody Big.

automatic, which proved as easy to handle as a live fish. Jack couldn't drive, Mum needed to rest, and I was scared. That left Dad, who launched us into a shuddering hundred-yard dash. Mum shrieked, 'Are you trying to kill us, man?' He tried again, but the automatic transmission and light-touch brakes got the better of him. He'd never had a sensitive touch, to which his wife would attest. 'Linda!' she screamed. 'Your father can't do it! Don't let him drive! Stop him! He's too old!'

Dad slammed on the brakes and we lurched to a violent halt. 'Do you want to do the driving, Davina?'

No answer.

'Well,' he said, 'shut up, then.'

We lurched off again, but within ten minutes, I was seasick and Jack, hopelessly miscast as the navigator, had his head on the dashboard. 'Dad,' I said, 'I think it might be easier if I drove.' The poor man felt like he'd failed, and he had. Never mind, he got to see the landscape, which was stunning, if a little too close on the left-hand side. I managed to get us to our first hotel in four pieces, where I immediately ran into my room and flopped on to the bed. A wisp of smoke drifted into my face.

'Jack, please don't smoke.'

'Look, Lins, I'm not going to give up smoking while your bloody parents are here.'

'There's always a reason.'

'And your parents are two damned good ones – just shut up, will you?'

'You're never going to stop. You're going to die!'

We fought until I started whimpering and he had to put his arm round me. 'I'm sorry, Bun,' he said gently. 'It's just, this is really getting to me, you know? And you don't seem to realize that your nagging is useless.'

'I don't know what else to do.'

'There's nothing you can do. I know it's a stupid thing to do to myself, and I'm going to stop, but not today, all right?'

'When, then?'

He pulled back and looked at me. 'You're a bit spotty, Lins. Have you been taking your pills?'

I burst into tears.

'Hey,' he said, 'I've got an idea. Let me do you up the arse. How about it?'

He settled for a blow-job. I didn't even bring up the usual excuse about my exceptionally narrow palate.

When it was over, we picked up Mum and Dad and walked to the end of the pier, where the sea-lions were slapping and honking. Then we trailed after Dad as he checked out every single restaurant. It was all seafood.

'Tell your father I'm exhausted.'

'All right, Davina,' he replied, 'can you be at peace?'

Jack carried Mum back to the first restaurant and we settled for seafood.

'I can't believe they don't have trout,' mused Dad.

The next day, we saw the Monterey aquarium, with its sea otters and filigree jellyfish. After lunch, we set off towards hotel number two. The luscious Victoriana styling had looked pretty online, but in three dimensions it was a nightmarish hodge-podge of competing chintzes – Dad gleefully counted seventeen different patterns in the lounge. I'd picked our room for the Jacuzzi, and Mum and Dad's for the fire. The cosy picture translated into a feeble electric gadget, installed because the room was an icebox, sharing only one wall with the rest of the building. When we went to check on them, the 'fire' had been whining at full throttle for an hour and the room was still Arctic. Mum lay in bed shivering, but when I ran to get some blankets from Reception, they gave me a blank look.[10] I suggested we swap rooms.

10 California – where people pretend to live in a tropical paradise, and shiver all winter long. Even if there's a decent heating system, it's turned off, because the power companies are privatized. Even in Moscow, you'd be warmer indoors during winter.

'No,' snipped Mum, 'it's too late now. Did you two get in the Jacuzzi together? I thought I heard you laughing . . .'

Our room must have been on the other side of that wall. 'No, no . . .'

Dad found cheese and crackers in the lobby, and brought a handful back for their dinner. Jack and I went instead to a Thai restaurant full of orchids, where I sat, unable to eat, my face wet with tears. 'I can't bear it, Chief!' I peeped.

'Well, neither can I. Your parents are really awful. I'm sorry, but they're the most miserable gits on earth. And you're pretty horrible yourself right now.'

'Cute hat!' chirped a passer-by.

'Thanks,' I said. 'Chief, I know! I'm sorry. But it'd be easier for me if you'd at least talk to them.'

'I cannot talk to them any more. Your dad's humming is driving me bonkers. And the more I see of your mum, the more worried I get about the future.'

'What do you mean?'

'You're turning into your mother, Lins. And, frankly, I'm terrified.'

'No, I'm not!'

What was he talking about? The little wisps that had emerged on my chin, forebears of dark, wiry bristles? The tiny red capillaries on my thighs that would one day blossom into a hideous purple road map? Patting my arm, he turned to the menu. 'Come on, try and eat something. Fried bananas, Bun – you like them.'

Back at the hotel, we lay down, our heads just inches from my parents'. We heard the desperate wail of the heater, Mum's moans, and Dad's deep, admonishing rumble. Still, it was a good excuse not to have sex.

When we woke up, it was Christmas. We walked through buffeting winds to a restaurant, right on the sea, with a stunning view of rocks, waves, birds, sea-lions, sky . . . Denied a child's portion, Mum stacked her food behind a napkin, complaining bitterly – she felt sick if she even looked at a full plate. Jack spoke only to the waiter, from whom he ordered cocktail after expensive cocktail. I felt guilty: my parents were spending more on this meal than they would on eating out for the next year. You'd never have guessed it to look at them, but they were being really sweet. Trying to crank some enthusiasm into my voice, I said, 'This is really good! How's yours, Dad?'

'Not bad at all. Rather large helping, but it's very good. I don't get decent cooking at home, you see . . .' He ran his index finger down Mum's nose and she jerked away.

'Ach, leave me alone.'

'Mum?' I asked. 'Is your soup nice? It looks yummy. Mine's lovely.'

'It's all right. There's far too much of it, though, and the roll's got bits in.'

The table talk dried up completely after the first course.

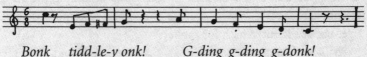

Bonk   tidd-le-y onk!   G-ding g-ding g-donk!

'Shut up, Alec. We're all sick of your noises.'

We sat, marooned amid the laughter and easy chat of the other families.

'They're having conversations,' observed Mum, sourly, looking at Dad. 'That's what you're supposed to do.'

'Is it really, Davina? I didn't know that.'

She took a sip of her water. 'That's what other families *do*.'

Dad put down his fork. 'Well, what do you want to have a conversation *about*, Bug?'

6: The Trouble with Everybody Else

'Your mother's your one true friend.'

Mum

Jack came home with a smile. 'Guess what Gayle said to me today? "Oh, Mr Stumford, I think you'd be the perfect husband!"'

'Well, you are, Chief.' I meant it, too: good looks counted for a lot with me.

'I suppose I am! What's for dinner?'

'You'll see!' I picked up a pack of photos. 'So, Chief,' I said, 'I got the shots back from my birthday . . . That's you throwing bottles in the fire.'

'What?'

'Yeah, it was really annoying. And this is you after you'd come out of the sea and rolled in the sand.'

He snatched it from my hand. It showed him streaming into the shot, eyes and mouth ecstatically agape. 'Oh, God,' he said, 'I look insane. That's really awful. I've made such an idiot of myself. Lins, I can't let myself do that again.'

'And there's you falling over on your way to the car.'

He gazed at it, shaking his head.

'I'm sorry,' I said, 'that I didn't get one of you throwing up.'

The doorbell rang. It was my friend Jacques, visiting from Paris. Jack went off to write while I finished making dinner. When he returned, the pair of them didn't seem to be getting along.

'Mmm!' squealed Jacques. 'This is delicious!'

Jack disagreed. 'It's not as good as she usually makes it.'

'I still think it's wonderful.'

'It's – I dunno. The meat's a bit tougher than usual.'

'Well, it tastes good to me.'

The conversation remained strained.

When we lay in bed that night, Jack said, 'You two seemed to be having fun together.'

'We are. Don't you like him? Are you just uncomfortable coz he's gay?'

'No.'

'Well, what, then?'

'You never laugh like that when *we*'re alone.'

Why was he surprised? I took for granted that I had more of a laugh with my friends than with Jack, unless we were play-fighting.

A couple of days later Jacques and I dragged my accordion to the top of Buena Vista Hill and sang my songs together. It was so beautiful – one quick scramble, and we were surrounded by trees, the undulating sweep of the city and, beyond that, the glinting seas. I felt suddenly brave. 'I'm sorry about Jack,' I blurted. 'He's just a bit jealous of how well we hit it off coz I never really had that sort of thing with him. My friends tend to be funny, and he's not, really, but I wish he didn't feel inadequate about it, coz, well, with a partner, you know, the relationship's built on something more than just hitting it off, you know?'

Jacques sat down on a tree-trunk. 'Linda, I have to say I don't agree with you.'

'You do like Jack, though, don't you?'

'I do . . . except he's so mean to you.'

'What?' I set up a vigorous defence, but he'd set my mind ticking.

Once Jacques had left town, I repeated the conversation to Jack. It didn't go down well. 'Why did he say that? What a cunt!'

I waited for a count of three. 'I think maybe he's right, though, a bit.'

'Well, of course you're going to believe him, you silly cow.'

'Come on, your mum's commented on it too – that you're so snotty with me.'

In a relationship you create an alternative reality, but I was determined not to be swept back into it. I clung to my opinion, and by three a.m. victory was mine. I also had a sore throat, a bloated face, a blocked nose and a headache from all the crying. Jack finally stopped calling me names. 'I'm sorry, Bun,' he said. 'I'll make an effort to make things better.'

Mickie was throwing a New Year party at a cabin in the mountains, and we were invited. There was a hot tub in the garden so I had to go. My parents never did anything at New Year except say, 'Thank God that's over,' so Mum didn't mind: 'You go and enjoy yourself, my darling,' she said. Another invitee gave us a ride to the party, and his broken heater really came into its own when we hit the mountains. When at last we arrived, I stepped numb-footed into the toasty cabin and made a frantic beeline for Mickie, dragging Jack behind me. 'Hi, guys!' The host smiled, then dropped his voice. 'Listen, you wanna take X with us?'

'No, thanks!' I said.

'Sure?'

I assured him we were sure.

'Not into that stuff?'

Jack said, 'Actually—'

'Cocaine, then?' asked Mickie. 'Little snifter with some crank?'

'No,' I said, trying to sound casual, 'it's OK.'

'Never mind. Come to the master bedroom.' He beckoned. 'There's something I want to show you.' A beautiful, wispy blonde rose from the bed and hung round his neck: Rickie, to rhyme with Mickie. She was twenty-one and recently widowed, having married a cocaine addict for the dental coverage (he had a job with benefits). The death had been a shock, but her teeth looked great. 'Yup!' beamed our host. 'I saw her on a date with another man, and each time she went to the toilet I followed her there and told her I loved her. It took me three times before I got her number. Didn't it?' She gave a Princess Di smile. Mickie certainly had an amazing ability with women. He once told me about his technique.

'I buy them drinks.'

'And then?'

'I buy them dinner.'

'And then?'

His hand grasped my shoulder, then moved down towards my elbow with a firm, rhythmic stroke. He held my gaze and smiled gently. 'You see what I'm talking about now, Linda? You really are so pretty when you're confused, aren't you now, eh? Eh?'

My defences were melting . . . Really, this was appalling.

The Stroker

When Mickie was a tender teen, he got some good advice:
When flirting with a lady, try to touch her (once or twice).
At first he tried some little prods, and then moved on to pats,
But since then he's become such a hands-on, close-contact, touchy-feely fella
That we really think a public warning's due.

They call him the Stroker – how can you resist
Those gently coiling fingers as they wrap around your wrist?
They call him the Stroker, it works every time,
Why not let those muscled hands commit the perfect crime?

They call him the Stroker, that's how he reels them in,
That and whispered promises of after-hours sin.
They call him the Stroker – one day he might choose you,
But when the Stroker strikes you then you know what you can do:
Look him in the eyes and say, firmly, 'I'd rather not today, thank you.'
And don't forget to give him a great, big smile.

'All right, Mickie, that's enough.' I'd snapped back to my senses and brushed his hand away.

'I like your skirt,' breathed Rickie, shyly. 'It's really cute.'

'Thanks,' I replied. 'Is that your real hair?'

As it happens, it wasn't. But before conversation had a chance to flounder, Mickie whisked her away, leaving Jack and me alone with the vodka. On the stroke of midnight, I kissed him and called home. 'Happy new year, Mum!'

'Happy new year, darling! Your father says happy new year.'

'Happy new year to him too.'

I hung up and trotted out to the garden to join the hot-tub frolickers. My shyness was cloaked by dark sky and hot bubbles, so it didn't matter that I had nothing to say. I smiled up at the star-studded heavens, and the outrageous luxury: snow and steam! It was so great I was almost happy. When my feet turned to prunes, I had to leave the warm embrace of the tub and headed back to the house for more strained chats with near-strangers. There, I saw no one I knew but Jack, who was out on the porch, balancing on the railing and flailing his arms. His drunken acrobatics scared me so I hid in the loo for a bit, then sat in a corner and began counting the minutes until people started going to bed. Mickie had invited us to sleep in the master bedroom, but when we got there, he was in bed with Rickie, two other girls, and another guy, passing round a little mirror and giggling.

'Oh!' I said.

'ARE YOU SURE YOU TWO WOULDN'T BE MORE COMFORTABLE ELSEWHERE?' screeched Rickie, her voice unrecognizable. It seemed we were no longer welcome.

'Sure,' I said, pushing Jack into reverse and closing the door on their laughter.

On New Year's Day, we greased our hangovers in a diner, then crunched our way through some enchanted scenery. There was snow below, mountains ahead, blue sky above, and I was miserable as sin. The moment people started leaving, I dragged Jack to the nearest car.

Back in San Francisco, Mum's grey face lit up when I came through the door. 'Did you have a lovely time, darling?'

'Yes,' I said, trying to sound excited. 'There was a hot tub in the garden, with steam coming out of it in the snow . . .'

'Oh, I'm glad you enjoyed yourself. That's what being young is for.'

'Mmm.'

'Not that you're so young any more.'

Four days later, they flew back to England, and all I had to remind me of their visit was a family-size Aero, a pair of oven mitts, three pairs of gloves, a blanket, a nylon sock and Mum's cold. My coping mechanisms collapsed, and I stayed in bed for the next three weeks. Jack went the other way, declaring that he now had the spiritual strength to effect absolute change. He held a glowing Marlboro at arm's length. 'See this?'

I kept on reading. 'Uh-huh.'

'Lins, look. See this? *This* is my Last Cigarette Ever. The absolutely last one. I'm killing myself, Lins, and I've decided it's got to stop.'

'Mmm.'

I paid more attention when he talked about sexy women. Usually, he spotted them on the street, but Mickie's Rickie had been a standout. 'She's really gorgeous, isn't she, Lins?'

'Mmm. It's amazing what you can pick up in a public toilet.'

'Come on. What's she ever done to you?'

'What do you want to do to *her*?'

'Christ, Lins, why d'you always have to be so nasty?'

It seemed too obvious and too complicated to explain.

I was riding the number 22 bus, minding my own business, when the man standing next to me cleared his throat. 'I hope you don't mind me saying this, but I see you on the bus from time to time and I really admire your style.'

'Thank you!' I beamed, and sat down in a warm glow.

But he hadn't finished. 'I think it's a gift to everyone who looks at you.'

Wow. If only Jack had agreed when I told him. But instead he said, 'Lins, can't you dress a little more sort of "modern"? Like Mickie's girlfriend?'

'What do you mean, "modern"?'

'Well, can't you wear a jacket, like something small, rather than those jumpers all the time? It's just that the stuff you wear . . . it's not very sexy, you know?'

'What do you want me to wear, then?'

'Just, sort of, you know, stuff that's sleek and fitted, not bulky and woollen. Like that.'

He pointed at a shiny black number in a shop window. I wasn't impressed. 'Do you want me to look like an extra from a sci-fi movie?'

It was a profound insult: my clothing was an accurate expression of myself – if I dressed like a slightly depressed misfit who wasn't out to catch a man, that was who I was. Jack didn't merely want me to dress more modern and confident and normal and sexy, he wanted me to *be* those things.

'Oh,' he said, sensing my indignation, 'forget it.' He put his arm round me. 'Your clothes are lovely.' Then he changed his mind. 'Let's get you some jeans, make you look more of a sexy Bun, show off that bottom.'

I hadn't owned a pair of jeans since I was eleven; looking 'good' wasn't my thing. However, I wanted to please him so I agreed. I enjoyed the attention: instead of wandering off to buy dope, he stood patiently by my cubicle and remained more focused and enthusiastic than I'd seen him in months. 'Go on, walk in front of me. Wow, look at that arse! You look great in those, Lins.' He picked his three favourite pairs and got me to wear the tightest home, walking behind me so he could admire the goods.

Sadly, changing my trousers wasn't enough. Shortly after this, I came home in my new jeans to find Jack staring at a piece of paper. He glanced up without smiling. 'You're looking a bit spotty today, Lins.'

'I know. What's that?'

He showed it to me. It was a two-hundred-and-fifty-dollar fine for smoking pot on the beach. 'Christ, I'm such an idiot.'

'Yup.'

'And we don't have any money!'

'Nope.'

'I can't do this any more. That's it, Lins – never again.'

I couldn't bear to think about it a moment longer. 'Do you want your potatoes mashed or roasted?'

Back in the kitchen, I started chopping away, singing the new tunes I'd been writing, my head sparkling with happy thoughts. Half an hour later Jack poked his head round the door. 'Please stop it. Please don't sing, it sounds really horrid. Lins, you haven't got a nice voice. And don't hum either, please. It's really annoying.'

I pinched my lips together and mashed the potatoes hard. 'Jack, everything I do seems to piss you off lately.'

'But your singing, it's awful. I can't stand it.'

'I know, I'm sorry. I hate it when other people hum, too, but it's not just that, is it? It's everything I do, especially since New Year. I can't believe I've suddenly become this incredibly irritating person. So is there something more, sort of, general the matter? Coz I'd like us to sort it out, rather than you picking on me all the time.'

'I'm not fucking picking on you!' He sat down. 'Look, I'm sorry, Bun. I have been picking on you. It's— You keep doing all these things that get on my nerves, and I don't know why I'm so annoyed, but, well . . .'

'What?'

'It's— Oh, I don't know. I can't really say this stuff.'

'What stuff?'

He sighed and began to light a cigarette.

'Jack, I thought you were up to two weeks this time. Please don't start again.'

'Just shut up, will you? God, you never give it a rest, do you?' I bit my lip; the fag-nagging was automatic. He took a deep drag and gazed up at the sky. 'OK,' he said. 'Well, you know, Lins, the way you behaved on New Year's Day, it wasn't right. I'm so used to being proud that you're mine but, you know, that day I didn't feel it any more. To be honest, I felt rather ashamed of you.'

My stomach was full of hot spikes. 'Why?' I asked, hunching over. 'What was I doing?'

'Like the way you spoke to Mickie.'

'I didn't know what to say. I didn't feel he liked me.'

'Maybe he doesn't, but it's not your job to fix it.'

I pulled my sleeves over my hands and folded my arms tight.

He pressed on: 'Lins, you don't seem very confident, and when you're like that, you act in funny ways . . . It's not nice to say it but, frankly, it's embarrassing.'

'Mmm.'

'You think you're a loser, and if you're a loser, that makes me an even bigger loser for being with you.'

As a child, I believed that if only I could be somebody else, everything would be OK. And I'd been right! But I couldn't dwell on the particulars because Jack had more to say: 'I'm happy with the way things are between us right now but, to be honest, I'm really worried about the future . . . and I see all these really attractive girls about, especially in this town. I used not to notice anyone, but now I do and I feel really bad about it.'

I was feeling really bad too, but I encouraged him to say more.

'After seeing what was going on at that party, I've been wondering about how things would be if I wasn't with you, and I could join in with stuff like that.'

'What – orgies?'

'*And* drugs, Lins. Anyway, I think it might be fun. I mean, I haven't taken drugs in ages. If someone like Mickie – I know he's really funny and everything, but he's not that handsome, is he? – if he can pick up a really gorgeous girl like that, well, it makes me think, What could I do?' He stubbed out his cigarette and flicked it into the garden. 'I'm sorry to say this stuff to you. I'm just being honest. I don't mean anything by it, Bun. But Mickie's so cool, you know?'

Cool? 'Cool?'

'Yeah . . . I want to be more like that. I need to have more space.'

Space: the final euphemism

We had a big talk and hammered out a deal that satisfied both parties: Jack would take drugs and fuck other people, and I would put up with it.

'It'll be OK, Chief,' I reasoned, 'because I know I'll remain number one.'

'Yes, of course, Bun,' he said, 'you'll always be number one. That goes without saying. But you can't rule anything out completely. It takes away the whole adventure of it. Know what I mean?'

I nodded, but in fact I didn't know what he meant. He flicked away a cigarette stub and began to roll a fresh one.

A couple of days later, he took off his wedding ring and dropped it into my sewing-basket. 'You understand, don't you, Bun? It would sort of . . . cramp my style. And it keeps on falling into the toilet, anyway.'

'Oh. Sure.'

He sighed. 'You're upset, aren't you?'

'Well, you know, it's just . . .'

'Christ, don't be so sentimental, Lins.'

Part Two: *The Muddle*

7: Jack Tries His Luck

> *'Be good to that boy of yours, Linda; you're a lucky girl.'*
>
> *Mum*

I justified his behaviour like this:

- He has to get it out of his system so he's not wondering 'What if?'
- He's earning the money so I don't have a choice.
- I don't want to be anyone's ball and chain.
- Wanting to cheat's as bad as doing it, so he might as well enjoy himself.
- It'll prove how much I care about him.
- It'll demonstrate that our relationship transcends sex.
- I won't have to have sex any more because these other people can do it for me.
- He's not actually going to be cheating because he's going to tell me about it.

I did feel a sense of dread, but that was silly, surely. After all, he kept coming home disappointed, and really pleased to see me after being with strangers who didn't love him. We were on a path of progress, and all would be well. Tra-la!

One night, we went out together to see a band and bumped into

Mickie and his troop. I found seats and Jack joined me, an excited look on his face. 'Hey, Bun, a *really* pretty girl just looked at me and said hello. She was so friendly! I think she liked me. Oh, she's there now.'

I looked over. 'Jack,' I said, 'that's Rickie – Mickie's girlfriend. The one you want me to be more like. You already *know* her.'

'Oh! Really?'

Sometimes it was sheer tactlessness, but mostly it was his drinking that spoiled things: he was a rambunctious drunk, and his lolloping scared people. I began to notice the forward-backwards jerking he did with his head and upper body when he'd had a few, especially in difficult social situations. It was a sort of pecking motion. Fearing, correctly, that his mind didn't turn over fast enough to generate dazzling repartee, he drank to quell the anxiety – better to be deemed an idiot than a bore. I hated it when people looked at him with disdain, and tried everything I could think of to get him to stop, including being nice. I also suggested a code word for 'stop drinking', which he respected on several occasions. Luckily I missed most of his drinking sprees because he was out on the pull.

As we walked home one night, he decided to climb up some rickety scaffolding and disappeared into the San Francisco mist, leaving me alone on the street-lit pavement. For a few minutes I called up to him foolishly, until I realized, with the echoing of my feeble voice, that I was yelping in vain, like a cat miaowing plaintively at the moon. I went home. He came back an hour later, talking excitedly about the people he'd met on the roof. Another time he went out to a club in a white top, which came back with an indelible footprint on the back of it. He had no idea how it had got there. Almost all of his clothing was decorated with bloodstains, rips or burns. I confided in a friend. 'Linda,' she said, 'Jack is an alcoholic.'

I disagreed. 'It's not like he's drinking a bottle of whisky a day. He can still do his job.'

'Listen. If alcohol is causing problems in your life that you can't control, you're an alcoholic.'

Back home, I suggested cautiously to Jack that he might attend an AA meeting. 'Not that you're an alcoholic, Chief, I'm not saying that.'

'So what *are* you saying, then?'

'That you could get some tips, meet some other people with similar stuff going on . . .'

'No . . .'

'Why not?'

'I don't want to go to a room full of people whingeing about their lives. And I don't have a problem – I *like* getting drunk. It's fun. Some of us like to have fun, Linda.'

I gave up. After all, what did he need AA for? He had his own twelve-step programme:

1. Have a drink.
2. Have a few more drinks, ignoring your wife's plaintive looks.
3. Begin to slur words and become overbearingly friendly.
4. When your wife asks you to stop drinking, shout, 'Fuck you!'
5. Disengage from your wife's embrace.
6. Continue drinking until walking requires concentration.
7. When your tearful wife pleads with you to stop drinking, shove her away.
8. Zigzag slowly home along the pavement and refuse to climb hills.
9. Where possible, attempt to climb scaffolding and/or large trees.
10. Refuse to get into bed.
11. Vomit, curse, get stoned, eat cheese (choose two).
12. Spend the next day in bed with a migraine, repentant.

Of course, there were times when he wasn't drunk, stoned, hungover, out on the pull or suffering from cigarette/alcohol withdrawal. On these occasions, he worked on his gloomy poetry and stories, or went roller-blading. Meanwhile I had developed a rash – a miniature mountain range of red bumps that ran across my forehead and down my cheeks. I went to the doctor, who took one look and said, 'Acne. Take these twice a day, wash with this three times a day, and rub this in at night. You'll see some improvement in ninety days. No sunshine or makeup.'

My glamour-rating was at an all-time low. I also had an impacted wisdom tooth and – perhaps connected – my love had developed a medical-standard hypersensitivity to my breath. If I came too close, he'd send me off to gargle, then sniff the result. 'Open wide . . .' I'd usually be sent back to the wash-basin a couple of times. One night I climbed on top of him while he was lying on the couch, reading, but he craned his head away from me, a disgusted expression on his face. 'Fuck off, Jack,' I protested. 'I've already mouthwashed twice.'

'Really? OK, then, come here.'

We had a little kiss and he took my face in his hands, with an adoring smile. Then his gaze shifted to my cheeks and he pushed me away. 'I feel really bad, Bun.' He sighed. 'I don't know what's happening to me. I've noticed that I like you more when your skin's better than when it's spotty, like it is today. How much longer before they said that stuff'll work?'

'Three months.'

'Mmm. That's a long time.'

'I know.'

'But, hey – I forgot to tell you – I haven't smoked a fag in twenty-four days!'

'Great,' I said, flatly.

'Yeah!' He took a sip of tea. 'You know, I'm really looking forward to it.'

'Yes, I'm sure you are.' Sometimes he struck me as repellent.

He peered at my face. 'Those hairs on your chin, Lins, they're not very nice. They remind me of your mum – could you do something about it?'

I did as he said. Martyrdom runs in the family, as well as bristly chins.

In my half-blind, flailing search for work, I picked up a gig accompanying a singer. The moment we met, I knew we'd be friends – it was like looking in the mirror, except someone had turned up the colour control.

Name: Heidi

Age: 30

Appearance: neon rainbow made of sticks

Philosophy: intensity in all things

Source: Nebraska

Occupation: singing and researching the sexual practices of gay men with HIV

Manner: awkward yet bold

Liked
- Swiss things (yodelling, fondue, etc)
- alcohol and women (formerly)
- Coca-Cola and men (currently)
- hand-stitched *c.* 1970s wall-hangings
- radioactive Fiesta-ware
- me, apparently

We rehearsed that weekend, and I loved her voice, which was sweet with a hard edge. She was dating a fat magician and working in academia, and didn't recommend stripping as a career: 'You know, I earned six hundred dollars lap-dancing at the Exotic Erotic Ball, but I had to spend it all on therapy to get over the trauma. That scene is just hideous. You have to hustle – going up to these disgusting men, who can reject you or grab you. That's where I met my boyfriend – I gave him a lap-dance and then he transformed me into his girlfriend. His best trick ever.'

Seized by a sudden daring, I asked if she'd sing my songs. 'You have just the kind of voice I'd imagined for them.'

'My old-lady voice?'

'Yeah!'

We began rehearsing in the subway, and soon I could get through most of the songs without stopping. Through Heidi's friend Duckbill Pete, we got our first real gig at a bar called the Odious – centre of all things strange and silly – opening for a death-metal *Sesame Street* cover band. This was exciting: I wanted Mum to know.

'Clunking Palsy twofivesevenfivethreenine.'

'Hi, Dad, it's me.'

He paused. 'Oh, it's you, Linda. Hold on, I'll get your mother.'

A little breathless, she picked up the receiver. 'Hello, darling, it's Mum. How are you doing?'

'I caught that cold you two had.'

'Oh dear, are you all right?'

'Yes, just a little tickle in my throat.'

'You must look after yourself, my darling. Are you warm enough? I worry about you in that place, without any central heating. Shall I send you a blanket?'

'You left one here, actually.'

'Oh, that's good.'

'How are you feeling, Mum?'

'I'm very tired, darling. The flight was too long for me. I don't think I can do that again, but it was lovely to see you, though I felt we overstayed our welcome.'

'Mum, I asked you to come! You were very welcome.'

She began to cry. 'I felt terrible, imposing on you.'

I felt terrible, too. 'How's the weather over there?'

'Oh, dreadful. It's freezing. My hands are white. My mouth ulcers haven't healed and my teeth are rubbing against my gums. They've rubbed them raw. I'll have to get new teeth, but the dentist said it would be nine hundred pounds! And I'm freezing – your father keeps turning off the central heating, and I've told him I need the place warm, but he never listens. I'm exhausted.'

'You should let yourself sleep in if you need to. It's fine.'

'But I have so much to do! I've got a huge pile of ironing, Linda. I've got to get myself organized.'

'You've got to get yourself better.'

'And you've got to get yourself working.'

'I'm trying, Mum. But in the meantime I've written lots of songs. I think you'd like them.'

'But what about work? You should be working, not playing the accordion.'

'I'm not too busy to work because I'm playing the accordion, Mum.'

'You should write a book, my darling. Look at that *Harry Potter* woman.'

I couldn't just write a book: what would I write one about?

To my parents, money meant security, and security meant everything, so when the bottom had fallen out of my career Mum wasn't interested in anything else I was doing. I was trying to do what she wanted, but all my applications had garnered me was half a day's work on a trucking logistics website. I felt guilty for not getting a job in a bar or something, but despite all the signals, I clung to the notion of myself as a copywriter. It was rather like Jack – something I'd struggled to get, and therefore refused to give up lightly, even though it didn't quite suit me. In the meantime, I carried on trying to earn some pocket money playing the violin, auditioning as a musician/sexy dancer for a horrendous big band that played Stevie Wonder covers. As they filmed my rendition of the dance routine,

I wished for a rapid death. Casting a doubtful look at my peg-legs, the lithe dance instructor said, 'Dick likes loose hips,' and sighed. At home, I demonstrated the sexiest gyration for Jack.

'How do my hips look, Chief?'

'Tight.'

'Not loose?'

'Really tight.'

Dick never called me back.

In March, my tight hips and I were invited to perform with Heidi at a big fancy-dress party. Jack came along too. After five days without cigarettes, he was in a foul temper, and we came to blows beforehand, over my bee costume.

'It isn't sexy, Lins. Why do you always have to make yourself look horrible?'

'It's a costume. They're supposed to be silly.'

'Why don't you take off the honey bags and wear that little skirt instead?'

'Because then I won't look like a bee, I'll look like a girl in a little skirt.'

'You'll look lovely. Go on, I'll help you with your wings.'

I agreed, on condition he wore the angel costume I'd made him. Unfortunately I'd been pushed for time, and bits of wire stuck out of his wings. They kept snagging on people's outfits so he'd be dragged backwards until he could disengage. 'Christ, Lins,' he griped, 'couldn't you have made the damned things more carefully?'

'Couldn't you have made them yourself?'

'I don't want stupid wings.'

'Well, you should have thought of another costume.'

'I could have come in my own clothes.'

'You really are a riot, Jack. A laugh a year.'

We were adrift in a dazzling blur of sequins. To me, it was a magical, dream-like scene, except I had to hang out with a sulking

120

angel dressed in a T-shirt and jeans and a distressed singer who was fighting with her boyfriend on her cell phone.

'He is SUCH AN ASSHOLE!' Heidi snapped her phone shut and wept.

At least the fucking-other-women plan was going well, considering that Jack wasn't getting laid – or anywhere near it. As I'd hoped, he now viewed me as an ally, rather than an encumbrance, and was revelling in his new-found freedom, even if it was only the freedom to hang around in bars looking at girls. It seemed quite possible that he'd give up. Arriving home one evening after rehearsal, I found a picture he'd drawn of a smiling bear with an arrow pointing to a pint of beer. Bear + beer = Jack out on the pull. I went to bed and started reading about string theory, but kept losing the thread.[11] He was out later than usual. Was this *the* night? Just after midnight the phone rang and the book shot out of my hands. Adrenalin soaring, I reached out and, after a pause, grasped the receiver. 'Hello?'

'Hi, Bun, it's me.'

'Are you having a good time?'

'No, it's miserable. I want to come home and be with you. You're the best of all.'

'Come on, then,' I said. 'I'll see you in a little bit.' I flopped back, relief washing over me like a smile, while he trudged sadly home, brooding over his failure. Almost two months, and he'd barely got anyone's number. What was wrong with him?

Half an hour later, he was under the covers with me, sharing his experience. 'I missed my chance tonight, Bun! There was this really sexy girl sitting on this sofa on her own, and I was just about to go and sit next to her, then two friends sat down on either side of her. I'm such an idiot. I've got to move faster. I mean, I've never done this before – I don't know the moves or what to say. I get all shy.'

---

11 String theory is the idea from quantum physics that the basic fabric of the universe is not particulate in nature, but consists instead of extremely fine spaghetti.

'But you're good-looking, Chief.'

'I know, but it's so hard, Lins. I feel like such a carnivore. And I never noticed before just how much of this goes on. Now I can see how all these guys are lined up, assessing the merchandise, hoping to make a swoop. It's really unpleasant. I never imagined it would be so difficult!'

Easy

I'm looking for a tarty girl, the kind no one respects,
Who wraps herself in shiny clothes and looks for casual sex.
I've spent whole nights on bar stools, nursing just one drink,
Not one of them came up to me. It really makes you think . . .

Oh, why is it so difficult to find somebody easy?
I only want the regular – nothing sick or sleazy.

I'm looking for a friendly girl, the kind who'll take me home,
Tie me to a table leg and cover me in foam.
I'm on a solo mission, searching for Miss Right,
A sweet, caressing angel, who'll do me for the night.

Oh, why is it so difficult to find somebody easy?
I only want the regular – nothing sick or sleazy.

I'm looking for a randy girl, the kind who doesn't mind
Waking up in strangers' beds with marks on her behind.
I've almost given up now, running out of hope,
It's hard to spend the night alone, but I'll just have to cope.

Oh, why is it so difficult to find somebody easy?
I only want the regular – nothing sick or sleazy.

*

'Thirty-one days, Bun!'

I looked up in disbelief. Surely not? Oh, no . . .

'Could you stand up and lean over the table this time? It'll give me a bit more leverage.' I gritted my teeth and concentrated on not screaming, which was hard without a pillow to bite.

Afterwards, he stepped back to check out my bottom. 'Hmm. Could do with some work, Bun. Must stop eating all those little rabbit treats!' He gave me a friendly slap and went out to make some new friends. Around three a.m., he staggered in, looking very pleased with himself. He'd gone to the Fulsome, a giant meat market packed with teenagers. 'I got chucked out by the bouncers! They said I was "bothering the ladies"!' He really seemed to think it was funny.

One night we went dancing together, round the block from our flat. The place was packed and, as far as I could tell, the music was pretty good. We bounced about for a while, until he bent down and shouted, 'I'm going to try my luck, Bun!' I nodded as he sped off. A few minutes later, he trudged back, saying, 'There's nobody here!' and I sympathized while smiling inwardly. Just then, he spotted a 36C brunette at the bar, and headed over. I kept moving my legs and arms on the dance-floor, waiting for him to come back, but they were still chatting when the place closed, so I slipped past and walked home alone. I told myself it was a relief – at last he'd bloody got somewhere and now we could move ahead. Then I noticed that I was breathing funny. By the time I got home, my legs were trembling. I froze in the corridor, holding on to my stomach – my feelings about Jack coming unbattened as the storm gathered momentum. It was happening, it was happening, it was—

'Jack?'

He closed the door behind him. 'Hi, Bun.' He sighed. 'No luck. She let me buy a drink for her and her friend, and then she told me she had a boyfriend and lived in LA.'

'That's a bit mean,' I said.

'No, she was really nice. You'd have liked her.'

'Er, I don't think so.'

It was soothing to dehumanize these people, and view them merely as things for Jack to fuck, but as Tina pointed out, 'They're women, just like you and me.' Each time he set off on the prowl I had wished him success – but from that night on, I meant it. At least if he was getting laid, we'd be moving forwards, towards the time when this nonsense would be behind us. That was my theory but, whatever I thought I was thinking, bitterness was seeping into my blood, drip by drip.

A week before Easter, I was able to test the theory when Jack got lucky in Golden Gate Park. He came through the door, roller-blades slung round his shoulders, face sparkling with sweat and elation, and, smiling, he handed me a business card:

Susan Jones, Pilates Instructor
Private and group tuition available
Movement for health and vitality!

I handed it back. 'Yeah!' he said. 'I saw this neat behind skating past and I followed it. She was wearing really pretty denim shorts; showed off her arse nicely, and I caught up and we skated up and down the pan-handle park a few times, and then back to her house so she could give me her card. And as she's a fitness instructor she's in, like, really great shape. I told her about you on the way there. I said, "By the way, you should know that I have a long-term partner." I think she was disappointed.'

'What did she say?'

'Well, she was quiet, and then she said, "So how does that work?"'

'And what did you tell her?'

'I said we're committed to each other but moving towards an open relationship.'

'Not really, Jack. It's only open at one end, like a sock.'

'You're free to find other people too.'

My guts lurched. 'Wouldn't you mind?'

'Why should I?'

Mind, damn you! 'But I don't want to.'

'That's not the point, Bun. Oh, it seems a shame to ruin things so early, but I don't want to lie to anyone. I need to come up with a better way of saying it. Anyway, it made things really tense and she said we can only meet as friends. I feel a bit bad about it, because she was obviously quite thrilled to meet me ... Perhaps this isn't going to work, Bunny. I don't want to hurt people.'

He decided to work on his spiel, putting his copywriting skills to practical use. It must have done the trick, for within the week he was out at a gig with the Pilates instructor. Despite her insistence that they were just friends, they missed the band because they were snogging, and the hot action didn't stop there. 'Wow,' he fizzed, when he got home, 'she's really into me! She actually straddled me in the cab.'

I couldn't share his enthusiasm. 'That's nice.'

'She really likes to use her tongue. Gets right in there, like right in the back of my throat. It's a bit much but, you know – good.'

'Uh-huh.'

'And she's incredibly supple. It's really weird feeling a different body. Her arse is totally muscular – it's, like, rock hard.'

Why did he have to go and find a goddamned athlete? Now her Olympian behind would be the gold standard by which all others were measured.

The following weekend they went skating while I fussed over an elaborate dinner. I wanted to remind Jack where the good stuff was – he was very emotional about his food. After his date, he was supposed to go to a weekend work meeting, but he never came back for his shoes. I assumed he'd blown out the meeting to stay with his Pilates instructor. Unable to eat, I put the food into the fridge and shrank into a state of suspended animation. Around ten p.m., he breezed through the door, grinning. 'Sorry I'm so late!'

I emerged from my cryogenic state. 'So, you didn't go to your meeting, then?'

'Yeah, I went.'

'Without your shoes?'

'Oh, I just kept my blades on. We stayed out too long skating, and I didn't have time to come back and change.'

In rushed my old friends Relief and Disappointment. 'Did you have a nice time, then?' I asked calmly.

'Yeah, it was a good meeting.'

'I mean with her.'

'Oh, yeah, we had a lovely time. We checked out the bison in the park before heading up to the Cliff House. She described them as hairy little clouds. Isn't that cute? We skated all the way – she's a really good skater – and in the end we went in the camera obscura, had a bit of a snog in there. You should see it, Bunny, it's amazing. And then she took me to a park I'd never been to before. Sutro Park – it's beautiful.'

'So what did you do there?'

'Skated around, you know . . .'

'I mean with her.'

He laughed. 'Let's just say there was a lot of snogging!' Oblivious to my antipathy, he carried on extolling her virtues. 'She's petite, and her breasts are even smaller than yours!'

I plonked down my cup of tea. This was too much. 'Jack, why did you tell me that?'

'Christ, Lins, I'm just trying to be nice to you.'

'Dinner's in the fridge.'

'Not hungry, thanks.'

A technicolour postcard arrived, covered with over-bright palm trees and vintage cars.

Dear Linda
I haven't been here and don't know how I got this card. Never
mind, it lets me say 'Hello' to you. How are you surviving this
week? I'm reading about Dürer for my class – so many
wrinkles! Lots of love, Mum XXX

My friend Smou[12] came to visit and spent most of the trip shopping – London must have been sold out. We hung out while Jack went off on a date with Susan. I was too ashamed to tell Smou what was going on, and hardly heard a word she said as imaginary scenes from the Date slammed into my mind. After all that, he came home, climbed into bed and went to sleep with me in his arms.

The next day he gave me the low-down while Smou was out in search of a pair of pink boots. I was having a bath, so I got the story with an echo effect. He'd invited her to the Tosca café. 'You'd like it. It's a really cool place.'

'How did you find out about a cool place?'

'I checked in the guidebook.'

'You've never looked in it before.' Work had given him a hundred-dollar bonus to take me out to dinner, and he'd never got round to it.

'Oh, leave it, will you? Anyway, she looked really good. She had on this silver mini-skirt.'

'Mini-skirt?'

'Yeah. You'd like the way she dresses – she looks really good. Like, the last time we met, she had this kind of leopard-print top on.'

I hate animal prints.

'Anyway, we were having a really nice time, and then she goes and spoils it all. She looks at me very intently and says, "So, tell me about Linda. What's the deal with you two?"'

12 A Pre-Raphaelite songbird, who had suffered in the rank-and-file of Cambridge Footlights comedy alongside me, Smou had an exquisite nose and a raucous sense of humour.

'So what did you tell her?'

'The truth, of course – what else? And when I'd finished, she said we were both being very naïve and that if we do this we'll end up losing the relationship. I don't know, maybe she's right. She's really wise, Linda. She said she wanted to have a casual relationship with me, but realized it wouldn't work because she had an awful feeling in her stomach when she thought about me. I asked her what I could do to make it go away and she said, "Leave Linda and move in with me."'

I wound up my clockwork trout. 'Why don't you take her up on her offer, then?'

That pissed him off. 'Because I don't want to live with her, Linda.'

'Why not? She doesn't hum all the time, I'll bet.'

'Look, I don't want to. And why should I move out? I'm the one who's paying for this place, for fuck's sake.'

'I'm just saying that maybe you should consider it.'

'For God's sake, you fucking silly cow, stop trying to make me move in with her! You can't do this to me – you can't rule my fucking life!'

I set the trout in the water and watched it flap around noisily. 'I don't see why you don't want to.'

'If you really want to know, she's older than you and not as pretty.'

For an instant, I felt better. But then I realized that, if it came down to those categories, I wouldn't stay long at the top of the pile.

On Saturday, Smou and I went out for lunch with Jack. *En route*, she went to check out some handbags while I went to photocopy my new songs. Jack followed me and stood by the photocopier. 'Why are you so different when you're with Smou?' he hissed. 'Why can't you be yourself?'

I lined up the edges of 'No Butts' and pressed 'start'. 'I am myself with Smou.'

128

Jack sighed. 'Look, Bun, I've been thinking – it probably would be best for us to live apart.'

I finished up, paid for the photocopies and went outside, where Smou was swinging her new handbag. 'What do you think, Linsikins?' she asked.

'It's great.' I was starting to cry. I couldn't be polite any more. 'Jack, we're going. See you later.'

'What the fuck?'

I whisked Smou off and told her everything, sobbing my way through a salad. 'Gosh, Linsikins,' she concluded, 'that doesn't sound like a very good plan.' I tried to explain why it was a good idea, but she didn't seem to get it. We talked for hours, and she returned me to good spirits.

When we got home, Jack was writing in the bedroom, and we stayed in the kitchen, cracking jokes and making dinner. I went to get him when it was ready.

'No, thanks,' he said, without looking up.

'Aren't you hungry?'

'No.'

'Why are you angry?'

'You two, you're like a couple of geese, cackling away in there.'

'We're having a laugh. That's what funny people do. They make each other laugh. It's not my fault you're not funny.'

'You're such a bitch, Lins.'

I started shouting: 'And you're such a tedious wanker, with your sententious fucking stories that never ever ever get finished.'

'Well, at least I'm trying to write something serious, not just slagging people off in rhyming couplets.'

But the food smelt so good he gave in.

Soon Smou went back to Britain and Jack went back out on the pull. He called at one a.m.

'Hi, it's me.'

'Hi, Chief.'

'I'm just calling to say I'm fine and I'm at someone's house.'

'Oh. A girl?'

'Yeah!'

'Oh. That's good.'

'Yeah, isn't it? So I'm going to stay here, m'Bun, and I'll see you tomorrow.'

'OK. Goodnight.'

'Goodnight.'

It had finally happened. It was as though I'd been on a roller-coaster, heading slowly to the top, click by click. Now I'd lost control and was hurtling down with the hurt and the shame of it.

He came home the next morning in jubilant mood. 'Bun?'

I was in the bath again. 'Yes?'

He bounced in, looked me up and down, said, 'You're so beautiful, Lins,' and spun round to peer in the mirror.

'What's wrong?' I asked.

'I've chipped my tooth. I'm not used to kissing another mouth!'

I seemed to have swallowed a bag of stones, and sank into the water.

'You'd like her, m'Bun, she's really grown-up.'

'Oh. How old is she?'

'Twenty-three.'

Well, I couldn't compete with that.

He told me all about it, and I was too stunned and too curious to ask him to stop. They'd met in Liquid Lust and she'd immediately guessed he was married, but still deigned to write her number in the large philosophy textbook he was carting around for toilet breaks. Not only that, she'd thoughtfully added a message for me:

Hi, Linda! Jack is my third married bastard.

'Thanks for showing me,' I said.

He missed the sarcasm and pressed on with his story. Once

they were back at her place, she'd made a huge fuss about the evils of married men before getting into bed with mine. 'She hardly ever takes people home,' he explained, 'and she's really shy with men.'

This didn't really fit the facts. 'How do you know all this?' I asked.

'She told me. She's so sweet, she didn't want to take off her shoes, and when she did she had to stand on tiptoe to kiss me. She's embarrassed about her weight, but she has no reason to be. I think she looks lovely. Nice arse too – it's quite big and very cute.'

She was soft and round and lovely and shy and sweet, and my bathwater was getting cold. 'What's her name?'

'Charlene.'

'Charlene?'

'Yeah, she's so different from you . . . She actually had a breast reduction! She was all embarrassed about it, and showed me the scars, saying, "There's something you should know." Her tits were still pretty massive, even after the op.'

She was bigger and better than me without even trying! 'So what did you do with her?'

He poked at his tooth some more, suddenly reserved. 'Let's just say I didn't get much sleep.'

I climbed out of the water, covered with goosebumps. Ten minutes later, I was knitting in bed. Jack sat down next to me, solicitous. 'Is something wrong? M'Bun? You're very quiet.'

'. . . Nope . . .'

'Are you sure?'

'. . . 'mfine.'

He lay down and started to kiss me while I carried on knitting. His touch was a welcome comfort so I let him slide his hand under my top and pat my stomach. Then he said, 'I've been with someone whose belly button is twice as deep as yours!' and I leaped off the bed. 'What's wrong, Bun?' he asked, bewildered.

131

'Why did you have to tell me that?' I snapped.

'Well, I thought you'd be pleased because she's fatter than you.'

I didn't care if she looked like a walrus.

It was perhaps ten days later, when we were sitting down to a roast-chicken dinner, that the phone rang. I answered and it went dead. Wow: a real, live cliché! I handed the phone to Jack. 'I think it's your girlfriend.'

'She's not my girlfriend.'

'You know what I mean.'

'Poor thing – she could be really upset. I'd better call her. Um – I'll take the phone into the bedroom. Thanks, Bun.'

I sat rigid before the cooling hen corpse.

Twenty minutes later, he came back. 'Sorry about that. She was upset, but it's all better now. Mmm, this looks delicious.'

'It's cold.'

'Aren't you having any?' I shook my head. 'Well, cold or not, it's still delicious. Thanks, Bun, this is lovely. You're a wonderful cook.' After he'd finished eating, he stuck on a video and put his arm round me. I didn't move, just stared at the screen numbly. He didn't notice.

As Jack was spending twenty dollars a day on lunch and nibbles, I had started sending him to work with leftovers. The following morning, a feast sat in the fridge, enrobed in clingfilm, but we started arguing over breakfast and he stormed out, lunchless. Tears streaming, I ran out after him in my pyjamas, caught up with him by the bus stop, and popped the box into his bag. He fished it out and threw it back at me, spraying chicken parts over the pavement. 'Keep your stupid lunch!' he cried. 'Who cares about lunch? Stop trying to control me!'

Tina's doorbell was right next to the bus stop so I rang it and collapsed in hysterics on her bedroom floor. She was kind and gave me a hug, and I was soon ready to go home and change out of my pyjamas.

Around noon, I got a call. 'It's me.'

'Hi, Chief.' I was so glad to hear his voice.

'Listen, I'm sorry, Bun. I was sitting here feeling hungry, and thinking about that scrummy roast chicken. I should have taken it.'

'So you're calling to say you're hungry?'

'Um—'

'Or that you were mean to me?'

'Well, both, kind of. It's just you always think about trivial things. You shouldn't have a packed lunch on your mind when we're talking about our relationship.'

I disagreed. A good wife is always mindful of the household budget.

In the midst of all this, my musical life was slowly taking wing. Heidi and I called ourselves Cotton Candy, and got a bass player:

Name: Tom

Age: 31

Appearance: beefy Cupid

Philosophy: I'll get back to you on that

Source: Wisconsin (Cheese Central)

Occupation: Michael Tilson-Thomas's poodle-walker

Manner: laid-back to melting point

Liked (aside from playing bass):
- his wife
- talking about how much he loved his wife
- spitting out of his car window
- estate sales, especially when the deceased had a size-seventeen collar
- his terrapin, Speedy

We were soon asked to play at a barbecue, and I agreed happily, envisaging a large, sunny deck with copious food and laughter. On the day, the organizer called me. 'What are you guys bringing?' she barked.

'Our instruments . . . ?'

'No, *food*. What food are you bringing? I'm not paying for all those greedy bastards! I lost a lot of money last time – you wouldn't believe how much they ate! Three or four burgers each! So this time the bands bring the food. Did I not tell you?'

'No.'

Just after noon I arrived empty-handed, and climbed up narrow stairs to a cramped back-room filled with acrid smoke from a foot-wide disposable barbecue perched on the fire escape. It could accommodate one and a half burgers at a time. Jack had brought along a massive steak for himself, but it was bigger than the barbecue so he had to take it home. I'd invited him to perform a song he'd written – a hunting-dog rap punning on the word 'bitch' – and he was anaesthetizing himself with drink and dope. 'I'm terrified, Lins,' he whispered.

'You'll be fine, Chief. Why don't you have a cigarette? That'll calm you down.'

'No, Bun, I can't. I'm nearly there. Twenty-nine days. I can't do it now. Lins, I feel sick. I'm just dreading this.'

His fears were justified. He could barely stand, let alone articulate the lyrics, and drifted across the stage until, by the end of the song, he was clinging to my shoulder. A smattering of applause marked the end of his showbiz career.

Charlene didn't call back, but the incident proved I couldn't handle the plan. I usually started wailing around ten p.m.: 'He dozzen love me any more! WaaaaaaAAAAAGGHHH!' Strays in the garden caterwauled in response, and Jack came through every hour or so to try to calm me down. Just before dawn I'd come to bed and curl up next to him – a poor choice for solace but no one else was available. He couldn't keep this up with his work schedule. One of us had to go, and I made sure it was Jack, arranging for him to sublet while a friend of mine was away. He's so useless, I thought bitterly, I even have to organize him leaving me!

'Me?' he gaped. 'Why should I move out? I'm the one that pays for the blasted place.'

'Because *you*'re the one who's upsetting everything.'

'That's such crap, Lins. It's your behaviour that's been upsetting me, and that's what's behind all this. And your constant bloody crying. How am I supposed to live with that? It makes me feel awful.'

'Well, boo-fucking-hoo!'

'You are such a cow, Linda.'

'Moo-moo! Jack – for fuck's sake, whatever the mitigating factors, you are the one who's actively being an arsehole. I mean, you *should* feel bloody awful.'

'Christ! Why do you want me to suffer? What good does it do you? This whole thing is terrible for me! You don't think about it from my position at all, and you keep trying to make me feel guilty.'

'Jack, you *are* guilty.'

'God, you stupid bitch . . .'

'I'm not stupid.'

'All right, then. Bitch.'

'Jack, you're going out trying to pull other girls, and I thought it would be OK, but it isn't. I'm not strong enough. I'm sorry, I didn't know.'

'And now I look like a total cunt. Thanks a lot.'

He moved into the sublet, but he couldn't pay for two places long-term so how would we live apart? I called him the next day with my ideas.

He said, 'I've already sorted it, thanks.'

I stiffened. 'You have?'

'Yeah. I didn't want this hanging over me. It's such a relief.'

'Oh. Um, good.'

He had a permanent place set up. 'So you stay in the apartment, and I'll come and get my stuff at the end of the month.'

'Well – OK.'

What the fuck? You push someone around in a wheelchair for years and one day the bastard gets up and *walks away*. In my mind's eye I saw Mum, discreetly finishing a chore, then crying, 'That's right, just stand there and watch me struggle!' I covered my face with my hands. Jack had been right – I *was* becoming my mother. I rented our bedroom to an uptight English couple, and moved into the living room. Tina lent me an inflatable bed.

I called Mum, hankering for some kind of consolation that she could no longer provide.

'Hello, my darling,' she said. 'I'm feeling terribly tired. I've got an awful headache, and your father's driving me up the wall. I can't stand it. He keeps turning down the central heating, and I don't know how many times I've told him . . . He's so mean! Now, how are you doing, my darling? Have you got enough money?'

'Yes, I told you, that job's going well.' To keep her happy, I'd exaggerated my connection with the trucking logistics website.

'That's marvellous, my darling, you keep plugging away. You must write a book, you must – look at J. K. Rowling! You always hide your light under a bushel and don't let people see your true talents.'

'Well, actually, me and Heidi, the singer, we're doing my songs around town, and people seem to be enjoying them.' I told her about a midnight performance we'd done on top of Twin Peaks, with the city lights arrayed behind us.

'Well,' she said, 'never mind. And how's Jack?'

'He's very well. He's doing a lot of roller-blading.'

'I'm glad you're both so happy, my darling. That's what Mother wants to hear. I'll let you go now, Linda, I'm going to miss *University Challenge.*'

'OK. I love you, Mum.'
'And your mum loves you too! Goodnight, my darling.'
'Goodnight.'

8: Confessional

'You've got to have someone you can trust in this life.'

Mum

Jack and I were living apart but I was still his best friend. As such, I got to hear about everything he was up to. I couldn't resist it, but each new piece of information stuck in my skull like a shard, a sharp edge that allowed me no peace. To help curb this, Heidi suggested I write a list of things I didn't like about him.

'I've found this technique to be very helpful, Lindy-loo.'

Once I'd started, I found it hard to stop.

BAD THINGS ABOUT JACK

- negative/morose
- dour relatives
- not witty
- naïve to point of cruelty
- never plans things to do
- spends spare time writing misogynistic, doom-laden poetry
- not a great kisser
- not silly enough when sober
- bad masseur
- aspires to promiscuity at age when most are moving on

- doesn't like my hands: 'a bit veiny'
- plays guitar; owns an electric guitar
- doesn't redeem ownership of guitar by practising
- throws spanners in the works in group decisions
- doesn't develop strong friendships
- dependent on drink, dope, cigs; likely to get cancer
- always goes on about his frail health
- bad knees constantly an issue
- oversize hips
- spotty bottom
- criticizes my bottom
- ten-to-two feet
- nasty toenails
- penile varicosity
- grumpy, esp. in morning
- cuts his hair too short so ears look big
- casts moralistic verdicts on me
- emotional state overly dependent upon my cooking skills
- constant reversals of opinions esp. re food ('I hate onions. Why do you always cook with onions?/I love onions. Huh? What do you mean? I've always loved onions, you silly cow.')
- can't remember anything
- shit about birthdays
- resists any celebrations, inc. our anniversaries
- can't drive
- refused to learn French
- turns vicious in arguments and calls me names
- hates me for making him feel guilty
- is guilty
- encourages me to sleep with other people
- unable to accept possibility of conflicting feelings
- prematurely wrinkled
- sullen when I'm with funny friends, then tells me off later

- makes pompous, nihilistic speeches
- twenty-four-hour post-orgasmic depression
- uses this as an excuse if I try to initiate sex
- angry with me for not initiating sex
- dependent (formerly) on me for all admin
- constipation
- consequent farting
- arms thin relative to thighs
- doesn't appreciate my clothes
- likes white underwear and dogs
- doesn't love me any more

Fifty-one reasons not to like him collapsed under the weight of the fifty-second, which tipped the scales and sent me back to square one.

The Fat Magician introduced me to another fat magician, who kept dropping his chainsaws. 'This is Linda,' he said. 'Her husband left her two weeks ago so she's gagging for it.'

I knew Mickie would be more sympathetic when I told him the news. 'So,' he said, smiling and rubbing my shoulder, 'you're on the market again, eh?'

I hadn't told my mum about the break-up; I knew she'd be more upset than I was.

'Hello, darling. I've got a splitting headache and I'm exhausted. I've been out in the garden, and your father just stands there watching. All he cares about are his bloody vegetables. What about the rest of the garden?'

I heard his voice in the background: 'I've told you, I'll do the garden, Bug, if you'll *leave me to it.*'

'Aye, and you'll kill everything there – you think all my plants are weeds.'

'Everything will be attended to in the usual efficient manner, without your yelping.'

'Ach . . .' She came back on the line. 'How are you, my darling? Are you warm enough?'

'Yes, Mum. So, what have you been up to?'

'I went to my Scrabble group. We had it at Mrs Branley's yesterday. She made lovely sandwiches, though needless to say I couldn't eat them.'

'How about the music classes?'

'Oh, they're marvellous. This week we had to take along something with the colour blue, so I took along *Rhapsody in Blue*, and next week it's ice so I'm taking that Sibelius you played in the orchestra. How's Jack?'

'He's great.'

'That's good. You've got a wonderful man there, Linda. You hang on to him.'

'OK, will do.'

I *was* hanging on to him – by a thread. This, I believed, was the only man I would ever want who would want *me*. The future without him looked cold and lonely, so I was determined to keep pulling on the thread. One day I'd haul him back in.

T&T kept buying me burritos and inviting me to watch videos. Their policy was to sweep emotional disturbances under the nearest rug; accordingly, I upped my dose of happy pills, giving my brain an extra layer of feather padding. I knew I was sad but I couldn't feel it, like when you bite your lip after going to the dentist. This anaesthetized me for my continued role as Jack's confidante. As he explored new realms, I stood at the threshold on tiptoe, tracking his progress and holding a plate of orange segments, waiting impatiently for half-time. One day, he called for a chat. 'Well,' he said, 'I finally got laid!'

'Oh.'

She was a tattooed, promiscuous twenty-one-year-old art student from Kansas, and 'quite cute'. I felt totally outclassed.

141

'Actually, m'Bun, it was kind of – awful.'

I rallied. 'What do you mean?'

'Oh, I probably shouldn't tell you this.'

'No, go on.'

'Well . . . Oh, it was . . . It couldn't have been worse in a way . . . God!'

'What?'

'It's so bad, Lins. She said that we didn't need a condom coz she was on the pill.'

'Jack!'

'Yeah, but I figured it would be fine because she looked so young and, you know . . .'

'What?'

'Innocent.'

'Innocent?'

'Yeah, I just assumed . . .'

'Was she wearing a white pinafore or something?'

'Lins, you know how it is.'

'No, I don't. So anyway – sorry – what happened?'

'Well, my – God – my frenulum[13] tore so I bled all over her, and to make matters worse she had her period, so if she's got anything I'll definitely get it too.'

'Hmm.'

'So, one fuck and I've got to have an AIDS test. I told her brother about it, Lins, expecting he'd say it'd be all right, and he's, like, "From what I know of my sister, you'd better get tested, Stumford!" I mean, Christ, if her own brother says it . . .'

'Good luck with the testing, then. Let me know when you know you're OK.'

---

13 *Penile frenulum. It's like the bit that attaches your tongue to the base of your mouth, but hung between the foreskin and the bit underneath. Not something you want to think about.*

'Thanks, Bun. Look, I'm sorry to dump all this stuff on you.'
''S OK.'
'There just isn't anyone else I can trust.'
'Hm.'
Gory action replays looped in my brain for a week.

Here's the silver lining: when your lover doesn't love you any more, friends remind you that they do. I received several heart-warming care packages:

- a wall chart listing my plus-points
- a poem declaring my greatness
- a poster of accordion players with 1970s hairstyles
- a skirt with a dartboard on it
- a fluorescent bikini
- a metallic green knitted suit

If only one could live on metallic knit-suits alone! Alas, I still needed a job. Jack was still paying the rent, so low pay would do – I could stave off sex work for a while. I kept my eyes peeled for 'Help Wanted' signs, and was soon conniving my way to a job in a costume shop. The owner was a half-wit megalomaniac called Tortelli; I handed over my CV – carefully stripped of A-levels, degree and professional jobs, then restocked with years of experience in non-existent shops – and he pored over it, muttering, 'Good, good . . .' He looked up. 'I'll be honest with you, Linda, I'm not looking for someone who wants to work here for a few months. I want someone who'll be here for the rest of their life.' I tried to look like that poor someone, gazing in awe at the overstuffed racks. 'Because,' he continued, 'this isn't straightforward work – you need the expertise and you need to love the clothes.'

'Exactly,' I said, and agreed to work thirty hours a week @ seven dollars an hour for the rest of my life, except it was tax free and, as

Tortelli pointed out, 'That's really like getting eight fifty an hour, isn't it?'

Naturally the job turned out badly. My boss liked to hover near the lingerie section and rushed over to 'assist' any woman who fondled his second-hand girdles, nylon slips and lacy bras. 'So,' he'd ask, 'what size are you up top?' With a staff–customer ratio of about four to one, we had to prowl about, looking busy, which is far more tiring than actually being busy. I'd pull things out of place so I could straighten them up on my next circuit.

On my first weekend there, a rowdy street fair was taking place outside. Jack lolloped in wearing a stained top and an unreciprocated grin. 'Hey, Bun!'

'Hi, Chief.'

'How you doin'?'

My back teeth clenched. He was drunk, and doing that pecking thing, swaying back and forth and bouncing on his feet. 'I'm OK,' I said quietly. 'Look, there's something I want to show you.' I pointed out a pair of corduroys with little carrots embroidered all over them. 'Do you like them?'

'Oh, Lins, they're sweet! Little carrots for a little rabbit!'

'I could buy them for you if you like. We get a staff discount.'

'Um, no . . . They're very charming but I wouldn't wear them. Especially now. It wouldn't seem right.'

I sank inside. 'Oh.'

'So,' he threw into the chasm-like pause, 'the move went well.'

'That's good,' I squeaked, trying not to let the tears fall out of my eyes.

He kept bobbing up and down. 'Feels really good to be out of it all, you know . . .'

'Out of what?'

'You know, us. Where's the loo, Bun?' He headed for a ragged curtain at the back of the shop below a sign that said, 'STAFF ONLY'.

Aghast, I grabbed at his sleeve. 'Please, Jack.'

144

'Come on, Bun, surely I can use the loo!'

Tortelli would be furious. I didn't want this drama at work. 'No, you can't. Look, can you just go away?'

'I only need a pee. Come on, Bun!'

'No!'

He yanked his arm free. 'Oh, piss off, then.'

He strode off, and Tortelli sidled over. 'Is that your husband?'

'Yes.'

'Seems a nice enough chap.'

'He was,' I agreed, 'until he started fucking other people.'

Tortelli didn't know what to say. He sidled away and I started straightening ties, my vision blurry with tears. Then one of the other assistants padded over. 'Do you know that man who was here?' she whispered.

I nodded. 'I'm married to him.'

'Oh!' she said, looking concerned. 'Well, I've seen him around. I saw him out with a girl. I'm sorry, but I think you should know.'

'What's wrong with him being out with a girl?' I demanded.

'Well, I mean,' she stuttered, 'it was definitely a date. I was kind of pissed at them for doing that in a club.'

'Doing what?'

'Kissing. I was thinking, Get a room! Anyway, that's why I remembered him, and he had this really bright pink shirt on.'

'Oh. Yeah.' Those fucking shirts! I'd made my humiliation into DayGlo public property by buying him all those tops in bubble-gum pink, sun-stripe yellow and so on. 'I know about that date,' I said.

She looked incredulous. 'You do?'

'Yup.' The tears escaped down my cheeks, and I walked off to the counter to organize the devil's horns.

When I got home I called Heidi. 'I don't know how long I can last there. It's so depressing. I have to ask permission to go to the loo, and all the clothes have different names, like jumpers are sweaters and dungarees are jumpers and pants are panties and trousers

145

are pants and vests are undershirts and waistcoats are vests. I had to put all the loose studs back into an Elvis costume by hand, about forty little metal stars. One of my fingertips started bleeding. And he said I'd arranged the fake noses all wrong. How can you arrange fake noses wrong?'

'There must be something else you can do. I know – why don't you teach the violin?'

'I'm crap at the violin.'

'Not as crap as the people you'll be teaching.'

She was right. It was a great idea. I wrote a glowing advertisement, and within the week, five students had signed up. The first was a glamorous young lady. I made her cut off her long French-manicured fingernails and never saw her again. But no matter: I had a production line going – a creaking machine with half-a-dozen saws screeching up and down, generating almost as much (or as little) as my costume-shop job.

I now felt strong enough to tell Mum about the break-up. I decided not to tell her about Jack cheating – if she didn't forgive him that would be awkward if we got back together. She burst into tears.

'Mum,' I pleaded, 'it's OK! There's no point in you being more upset than me.'

'Why did he leave?' she sobbed. 'Was he seeing other women?'

'No, we just weren't getting on well.'

'Because if he was, tell him your father will come over and skin him alive!'

I pictured my dad looking up from his crossword, specs propped on his nose. 'No, Mum, it's nothing like that. You know, we'd been together a long time.'

'It'll not be for good, will it? You should keep hold of a lovely lad like that.'

'Mmm.'

'So why did he leave you, then?'

'He didn't leave me, Mum. I told you, we agreed to part.'

'He's the one who moved out.'

'That's coz I asked him to, Mum. He was being nice.'

'It's not nice to leave my little girl. How dare he? What did you do to upset him?'

'I didn't do anything.'

'Come on, Linda, you must have done something. Your mother's not such an old fool, you know.'

I bumped into him next on the street by the cash machine. 'Hi, Chief.'

'Oh, hi,' he said, awkwardly. 'How're you doing?'

'OK. You?'

'Yeah,' he said, joggling up and down on his toes. 'Yeah, er, it feels really good to be living apart, you know? Come on, Lins, don't get upset – it was awful, you know that. Anyway, my new flatmates are really nice. They're very sympathetic about my situation.'

I looked up, bewildered. 'Sympathetic?'

'Yeah. You look after yourself, OK? Come here.' He drew me in, intending to comfort me, but recoiled when he kissed me goodbye. 'Ooh, pond breath! You really should go and brush them, Bun, or you'll never find anybody else ... Don't cry! Christ, you're always doing this! I'm just trying to help you.' He strode off in disgust. Except for a month I spent working the sausage machine in a meat-packing factory, this was my all-time low.

Tim and Tina had been looking after me all this time – checking in, inviting me to see films, printing my ever-changing CVs. When they invited me to live with them in their new place, I jumped at the chance. The only clear immediate problem was Tina's radioactive cat. You couldn't touch him without oven gloves, and he was always stimulating himself in my cupboard – the only time he ever purred. He insisted on sleeping on my bed, and if I closed the door on him, he'd caterwaul and claw until I gave in. Each morning, I awoke to a pair of bulbous, yellow eyes. Thinking it might be lonely, Tina asked me to get a cat of my own, and I hot-footed it to the pound. Instead of the Dickensian hell-hole I'd had in mind, the place was impossibly chic, and each kitty lived in a sort of miniature hotel, complete with room service. I stood shyly before a stuck-up Siamese, but Tina shook her head.

'No fun.'

The regular cats were a bunch of ancient mogs, all bullet holes and eye patches, but then Tina grabbed my arm. 'Here, what about that one?' she said. Soon, a cross-eyed kitten was perched on my shoulder, purring and licking my ear, its tail whipping across my nose.

'OK,' I said, my mouth full of fur. 'I'm in love.'

'What are you going to call it?' asked Tina.

'Madam,' I said, shutting my new love into her travel box.

The next unexpected source of misery was the temperature of the new flat. OK, it was on the ground floor and faced north, but its damp, cloying chill had a supernatural intensity – it was colder indoors than out. Unfortunately T&T were far sturdier than I. I tried to explain that it was as though we were underwater but they had wetsuits on, which didn't go down very well.

'And what are our wetsuits made of?'

'Yeah, what are you saying?'

Meanwhile, my blood was congealing. Though I wore tights, thermals, two jumpers, a hat, gloves and a coat indoors, I couldn't feel my hands and my nails were always blue. They gave me micro-wavable gloves to heat my hands before I taught my lessons because they didn't want me to turn on the heating. The system warmed up the entire place so it cost a fortune, and every time I flicked it to 'on' Tina flicked it straight back. I mentioned this on the phone, and Mum reminded me frantically that her circulation disorder was inheritable: 'You've *got* to keep yourself warm, my darling! Don't end up like your mother!'

While she looked out mitten patterns, I begged for mercy. 'Tina, *please* can we have the heating on a bit more? I'm cold *all the time.*'

'Well, put some weight on, then.'

That winter, I struggled to maintain my body temperature at night, beneath two feather duvets and an onion-like clothing system. Sometimes I'd masturbate just to get my circulation going. I had a hot-water bottle, but I keenly missed my human one, especially when I heard my flatmates giggling through the wall – on and uproariously on. They were trying to have a baby. It sounded like a lot of fun. Up above, the resident butch dyke slammed on the ceiling with the authority of a woman possessed of a large, resilient strap-on, making my light fixture creak from side to side. The cats curled up on the bed, and in the midst of all this love, I clung to an acrylic moose.

Moose

Through the wall a loving couple
Giggle, cocooned in their joy.
On my bed two black cats cuddle,
The girl has wrapped herself around the boy,
And here lie I – a girl and her plush toy!

Oh, Moose and I are happy together,
Moose will never break my heart,
Our union will last for ever,
And forever's a good place to start.

The couple curl up naked, glowing
Softly, their slumbers beguile.
Through the wall their dreams are flowing,
The cats are warm and cosy in a pile.
And here it might as well be snowing,
I'm in hat, sweatshirt, pyjamas single-style!

Oh, Moose and I are happy together,
Moose, you are my choice.
When you take me in your arms I feel such pleasure,
When you nibble my ears I rejoice.

Through the wall the loving couple
Make noises I cannot mistake.
The lesbians above seem very supple –
Their acrobatics make my ceiling shake.
And here lie I, indisputably awake.

Oh, Moose and I are happy together,
Moose will never let me down.
He's not an impassioned lover,
But then what is love? Just a noun.

Jack called to say he'd passed his AIDS test with flying colours, and added that since the all-clear he'd been speaking with his new girl every night. In a couple of weeks, he would be flying out to Kansas for a week of interactive training in the art of Bondage, Discipline, Sadism and Masochism. This was like flying from Spain to Scotland for oranges, but I didn't feel like laughing – he'd found himself a sexpert and I'd soon be forgotten.

I didn't have long to wait for the low-down on his sex holiday.

'Hi, Lins, how you doin'?'

'I'm OK. How was Kansas?' I braced myself.

'Oh, it was bad, Lins. Worst week of my life.'

'Oh . . . !' I tried to keep the joy from my voice. 'Why?'

'Well, she was busy with college and didn't take any time off to spend with me so I was stuck in her apartment all day, which smelled really badly of cat-shit, and the sex didn't work out. I kept going floppy.'

'Oh dear.' Bingo!

'I reckon she decided I wasn't as sexy or as cool as she'd thought, and she just didn't have time for me. I felt really pathetic.'

A pity-pang muted my jubilation. 'I thought you were going to try out bondage and stuff?'

'Well, that was a bit of a disaster. I mean, we did something with a rope, and she seemed to get really turned on when I put my hand over her mouth, but maybe she couldn't breathe. And she dressed up as a schoolgirl . . . Well, it was embarrassing, really; silly acting. At the time I blamed myself, but I'm thinking that maybe I don't find her that attractive, you know? She's really cute facially, but kind of, well, stumpy. Her legs are short. I guess I'm used to you . . .'

When we said goodbye, I patted my legs. I may not have loose hips . . .

At the end of the year Jack's luck changed, and he got exactly what he wanted for Christmas. First, he got laid off – a $3000 leaving bonus and $330 a week in unemployment benefit – and then he got laid again. On 23 December, to be precise, the night before he was due to fly to England. 'She's really nice,' he told me. 'I think you'd like her. And she had the most enormous arse. It was incredible, really incredible.' Sadly, the heady blend of speed, dope, cocaine, alcohol and sex had so muddled his head that he'd missed his flight and paid a surcharge of £250 to spend Christmas Day on various planes. After a twenty-seven-hour voyage, he arrived on Boxing Day in the UK where, as there were no trains running, he decided to pay £350 for a fifteen-minute flight from London to Manchester, obliging his aunt to make a six-hour round trip to pick him up. Hearing this story, I began to boil, but then I recalled that I was no longer his PA, and the rage evaporated. What a relief! I wished I'd resigned years ago, but it seems that in life I'm incapable of moving on voluntarily – I have to get myself fired.

Calling Mum, I wove a careful fiction of sunshine, cats, friends, sparkling conversation and good times. She burst into tears. 'I feel so sorry for you, my darling!'

This wasn't helping. 'Mum, I told you, I'm fine.'

'You've got no money and your husband's gone off. You've nobody to look after you! You're all alone! And cold! You mustn't be cold – can I send you a blanket?' We agreed on mittens. 'Linda, is there any hope?'

'What for?'

'Your marriage, of course.'

'Mum . . .'

'Oh, darling, your mother's frantic about you!'

'Don't cry, Mum. We're getting on much better now. Maybe things will work out.'

'Oh, I do hope so. I love you, Linda.'

'I love you too.'

'You don't need to be rich, but you need enough to get by.'

'Mum,' I protested, 'I have enough to get by. I've got some violin students and Jack's still supporting me. Will you please stop talking about money?'

'I just want to make sure you're all right.'

'Look, maybe there are other aspects to my being all right. Don't you want to know about my music or my friends or anything?'

'You must learn to think about the practical side of life before you worry about anything else. You *must* have enough to live on. So, darling, tell me, is there any word from Jack? Do you think he might take you back?'

Right on cue, she broke down. I asked her what was wrong.

'It's just, well, it didn't last very long, did it? Mildred is out there showing off about her Dawn and how she's getting a new Jacuzzi and they're going to have another grandchild and I don't know what to say to her!'

'Mum, impressing Mildred is not the guiding principle of my life. I'm sorry for mucking up your PR programme.'

'Mother always says the wrong thing! I don't know what to say to you these days.'

'How about being nice to me instead of upset all the time? Look, I have to go now – I have a student.'

'I'll let you go then, darling. You don't need your old mother wittering on at you – what do I know? I'm just an old biddy. Look after yourself and remember that Mother loves you.'

A few days later, an airmail letter arrived with strands of mohair attached so I could choose the colour of my mittens.

Jack's split with the Kansas art student had given me fresh hope. We had a rapprochement, and when he moved to the drug slums at the foot of the Mission district in the geographical centre of the city (a true hot spot), I went round to inspect the premises. What I discovered there made me uneasy – sex and drugs were freely available, courtesy of his new room mates: Colleen, an unemployed sales rep, and Amanda, an Irish cocaine dealer. During their many coke-fuelled parties, Colleen proved to be a proper five-a-week slag but, as she revealed over dinner, there were things even she wouldn't do.

'Ooh, I haven't swallowed in *years*.'

'Me neither,' agreed Amanda. 'Makes me wanna vom. This spag Bol's fab, Jack. Whatcha put in the sauce?' She was a sparky, raucous girl who loved to shout abuse at her friend: 'Colleen, you should scrub out that box of yours, you filthy tart. It's disgusting, the way you carry on!' What a scene. Condoms and full ashtrays littered the place, and they used old magazines in place of loo paper.

Jack said, 'It's "real" – know what I mean, Lins?'

'It's "real" scratchy, all right.'

Just then his flatmates exploded from the bathroom in their Friday-night best. Colleen wore a tight, white T-shirt (no bra) and stretch snakeskin mini-skirt, with her usual six-inch platforms. Amanda had the same shoes and a stretchy black catsuit with zips running up the legs and down the chest, all of which were completely undone. She looked like she'd walked out of a Bond movie for small people. 'Now, Linda, be honest,' she implored, 'do we look tarty?'

'Yes, of course,' I said, but that didn't seem to be the desired response.

They'd picked Jack to be their new flatmate because they both wanted to fuck him – Colleen confessed as much one night as she climbed into his bed. 'I just want a cuddle,' she'd said and, to her indignation, that was exactly what she got.

Jack had held back, but he admired her attitude: 'She's experienced so much, Lins, because she's out there and willing to open up to all kinds of people and situations. She really knows what she wants, and she's doing it.'

I felt threatened and disdainful at the same time. 'So what she really wants in life is to lounge on the sofa all day watching TV, steal food from her unemployed flatmates, have sex only when she's smashed and change partners every few days so no one even gets to know her surname?'

'You're so uptight, Lins. Get a life.'

Despite conversations like this, I continued to seek comfort in his ambiguous hugs. Alice – the cute Catholic best friend – reprimanded me from across the Atlantic and I promised to stop seeing him, but the next day I went over and slept with him.

'Wow, Lins,' he enthused, 'you seem to be, you know, *enjoying* yourself.' And then, in the precious, safe moments of Afterwards, he pulled out a photo of the S&M girl from Kansas.

I sat up and stared. 'Why are you showing me this, Jack?'

'I thought you'd like to see how she looks.'

'She looks like a toad. I'm going now.' I didn't want to go outside, but I couldn't stay with him and his toad picture. At three a.m., no one was about except shadowy figures in puffy coats, and his filthy duvet had triggered my asthma. I wheezed all the way home.

The next time I saw him was at a Cotton Candy show, at the Odious. Mickie was there, with all his friends, and Jack was trying to fit in, drinking and feeling awkward. During our set, I noticed some sort of kerfuffle in the crowd. Jack seemed to be looping masking tape round people near the stage, and tying them into a big, sticky web. From the look of it, he was pissing people off. My fingers drifted. I knew I shouldn't caretake, but . . . 'Chief, stop it!'

With a big grin, he gave me the finger.

Heidi: '*I'm looking for an easy girl, the kind no one respects . . .*'

Linda: 'Jack, stop it!'

He'd thrown a lump of rolled-up masking tape at me. When the song ended, I hissed through the mic: 'Jack, will you fucking calm down and stop fucking chucking stuff?'

Heidi ignored the masking-tape barrage. 'And for our last number, we'd like to do a song about Linda's first landlord in San Francisco. I'm sure many of you have suffered in similar ways . . .'

Tom: 'Three, four—'

Heidi: '*My landlord doesn't live here, and that's a piece of luck, coz he isn't very fussy about what he likes to* – cut it out, Jack!'

This time, he'd thrown the entire roll, knocking off the plastic canary I'd carefully woven into my hat and he was the only one laughing. When we were done, he came up and encased me in a big, sweaty hug. 'Hello, m'Bun!'

I wriggled free. 'No, Jack.'

Then he thrust me aside. 'You fucking bitch. Fuck you!'

I went to the loo to cry, but there was a queue.

9: Finding a Man in a Haystack

'For God's sake, Linda, sleep with someone before you marry them. You must know what you're getting yourself into.'

Mum

For 2002, I had resolved to get Jack out of my head, to which end I took a deep breath and plunged into the humiliating world of online dating. To prepare myself for all the great sex I'd be having, I stopped taking Prozac; there was something depressing about being on anti-depressants.

Aware of my tendency towards hero-worship, I wanted an older, uglier sort of man. One week after posting my ad, I found one: '31, Writer, 6'1"'. In the little pic, he was bare-chested, displaying some nasty tattoos, but I figured he'd be wearing a shirt when we met. We arranged to meet in a café, but when I arrived no one fitted the description. I sat in the shadows, heart thumping, and in trundled a bodybuilding type with a shaven head. He had some kind of rash on his scalp – it was bright red and splotchy. Was that him? With a sinking feeling, I walked over and smiled. 'Hi! Are you Brad?'

'Yeah – Linda?' His voice was a thin squeak.

'Yes. Pleased to meet you.'

The moment our hands met, my heart-rate crashed back to normal. On closer inspection, his scalp psoriasis turned out to be a red and black tattoo, augmented by acne round the forehead. I suggested we go for a walk so as not to waste the entire afternoon. At least I'd get some exercise. He agreed, and lumbered behind me, striving to make a connection.

'You're from Australia, right?'

'No,' I said, patiently, 'a long way from Australia.'

'Oh, right. New Zealand.'

'No, a really long way from Australia. The only place further away is the moon.'

He shook his head. 'You got me.'

'Scotland.'

'Oh, yeah! That's a nice town.'

He followed me up a steep and beautiful hill, and through persistent questioning I discovered that he was not technically a writer but earned his living building conference booths.[14] There's nothing wrong with that, but there's something wrong with keeping it a secret. He kept mentioning how strong he was, in case I hadn't noticed, and told me he loved to do 'really dangerous stuff, like jumping out of a hotel window, five floors up, into a swimming pool!' I tried to sound impressed, but all that came out was a dull honk. We had nothing in common except our taxonomy.

On and on I climbed until we reached a plateau, where we stopped to take in the view. In contrast to our conversation, it was magnificent. Beyond the clustered city lay the bay, a gorgeous swathe of blue, dotted with tiny boats; on the far side, more buildings sprouted behind a delicate veil of mist. Suddenly a large, hairy arm blocked out half the sky – my date was pointing at something. 'That's where I live, by that jutting-up bit.' I could just about make out a distant, shadowy bridge.

'Why do you live there?' I asked.

He thought for a moment. 'Well, the parking's good.'

---

14 British people tell you what they do for a living, and then make covert references to their hobbies or passions. Americans do the reverse, unless they're a doctor, an architect or a magician.

'So your ideal place to live would be a car park?'

He thought I was joking. I turned to descend the hill and he followed me down, taking my hand at the bottom, and saying, 'I'd like to see you again, Linda.' I was dumbfounded – how could he possibly have liked me?

I did have a sort of happy new year, because I was being paid. Heidi and I played classical arias at a strip joint, where we shared a dressing room with an annoying Russian acrobat who ran to and fro, crying, 'Hass anyone seen my dreell? Oh, my Gord!'

Apparently, her act consisted of climbing a ladder of swords while wearing a metal bikini, then making sparks fly from her crotch with a power drill, but by the time she was on stage, we were in a car with a sword-swallower and his wife, *en route* to gig number two, a private fetish event. Our hostess had massive hi-gloss lips, which she alternately pursed and opened, pursed and opened, revealing a writhing tongue in a wet mouth. I found this air fellatio unsettling, but forgot about it when we bumped into Heidi's friend Crazy, who'd come as an intergalactic warrior princess.

Name: Geanine, a.k.a. Crazy

Age: 25

Appearance: average bod, beautiful face

Philosophy: FULL ON

Source: New York

Occupation: fashion designer/ fairy princess

Manner: intense and hyperactive/paralysed with morbid despair

Liked:

- tofu
- talking enthusiastically
- complimenting herself and others
- swirling others' lives into disarray

'Wow,' I said to Heidi, 'she's very friendly. Why do you call her Crazy?'

'You'll see!'

Crazy introduced us to her 'make-out friend' Mitzi, an adorable nymphomaniac who was 'dressed' as a naked unicorn. They were discussing another stripper: 'Her entire life is about sex! Apparently she had a really terrible childhood, like so fucked up you wouldn't believe it, poor thing. But, nonetheless, she's totally cuckoo.'

'She asked me to do a speculum show with her once,' said Heidi.

'A what?' I asked.

'Some guys are really into it. They want to see your cervix.'

'Isn't it dark?'

'You use a flashlight,' said Crazy.

'Well, anyway, some guy requested it. She wanted me to slide the speculum in, but she kept saying, "Don't pinch me!" so I told her to do it herself.'

'You know she made eight hundred dollars at the last Exotic Erotic Ball?'

'No!'

'Yes, but she won't tell anyone what she did in her booth.'

'I know what she did,' said Mitzi.

'What?'

'Stuck a beer can up her butt.'

Just then, the annoying acrobat turned up, strangely lacklustre. I noticed silver duct-tape round the top of her thigh. I asked her what was up. 'The bladdy dreell slipped!' she cried. 'But 's OK, I've been patched up!' And with that, she did her entire act over again, blood clotting beneath iron pants.

As we sat together after the performance, a giant transvestite waltzed through the door. 'Hi, Fucchi!' called Heidi. 'How are you?'

The newcomer toddled over and sat down. He had stellar cheek-bones and the best pout I'd ever seen, which lessened the impact of his fifty-plus years. 'I'm the freak-*du-jour* at the Odious. They love me there. I'm doing thirties torch songs and I pack the place. I draw tears. I'm going to hire an accompanist. I want an accordion . . .' He turned to me. 'You play the accordion? We should talk. Oh, I suddenly have so many friends. They're all so kind to me there – all those gorgeous people like Mickie. He loves my act. Do you want to know who's on my love list? I'll tell you. Well, there's Rickie – oh, she is beautiful, but she's everybody's lover, and there's Robyn and Ben and Lucy and—'

'I haven't seen you in a while,' interrupted Heidi.

'I've spent the last six months homeless, my dear. It was absolutely dreadful. I don't want to talk about it. I've become very violent. I mean, nobody bothers me – I'm six-two, I'm very strong, but it was utterly miserable, utterly miserable . . . I moved into a place last month and it is wonderful, absolutely lovely. It's in the Tenderloin,[15] but that's OK. You just get used to the fact that you don't talk to anyone – *anyone* – on the streets. I slept rough, on the beach mostly. I didn't go to the shelters because the types who go there now . . . raise your voice and they're at you with a knife. They're terrifying people.'

He was off heroin and on hormones instead, but it was a struggle.

'I find it so hard to keep appointments and fill out forms. I was at the front of the line in the clinic and they were saying they couldn't give me my hormones, I hadn't filled out some form or other or something, and I just *lost* it. I said, "Give me my fucking hormones!" and they said, "Calm down, lady, calm down!" I think they'd have thrown me out of there but I said I was sorry. One day I'll smash a window, but so far I've just said sorry. Oh, and I need new boobs too.'

Heidi reassured him. 'Those ones look good, Fucchi.'

'No, dear. They've been fine for eighteen years, and they still have the right shape, but up here they don't have the right texture any

15 The most run-down and dangerous part of the city.

more. It feels like porcelain. But a new pair – that means hard cash . . .'

'Then perhaps you could get little ones fitted instead?'

'Maybe . . . I can do anything, anything. I know it all.' He gave us a twirl, saying, 'See how fabulous I look?' and stalked off into the night.

Heidi turned to me. 'Much as I love Fucchi, Lindy-loo, I don't recommend that you play the accordion with him. It's not a good personality fit.'

I could see what she meant.

When Heidi found out that her boyfriend, the Fat Magician, had paid everyone else twice as much as us to perform on New Year's Eve, she finally broke it off with him and retreated to her rainbow bolthole. There, surrounded by brilliant tapestries, glassware and soft toys, she watched endless musicals while love passed by. She lost weight and shaved her head, and somebody asked me if she had cancer. At rehearsal, she sang lying down on the couch, her voice a lifeless drone. She spoke compulsively about her failed love life, voicing the thoughts over and over.

'You know, Lindy-loo, I've dated – in order – asshole, crazy person, asshole, asshole, crazy, crazy, asshole, crazy, asshole. One long string of disasters! What is it about me? Why do I get together with these people? The idea of going on a date ever again makes me feel nauseous. And now I'm tainted – I dated the biggest pervert in town and no one else will ever want me . . .'

'Come on, there must be worse perverts in this town.'

'Don't you know about Udder Lady?'

'Who's that?'

'This lady who's always at the Exotic Erotic Ball. She's so gross, she's about sixty and her tits go down below her waist – I'm serious! Her husband leads her about on a chain and she gives out free blow-jobs, which is totally illegal – you're supposed to charge for services there. Anyway, my ex-boyfriend actually fucked her, right there in the hall.'

'He did?'

'I said, "How could you do that?" and he said, "Her husband asked me to!" As if he's ever given a shit about what anybody's husband thinks.'

She wiped her eye on a vermilion sleeve.

The next morning, I was repotting my spices when the phone rang.

'Linda? It's Mum. Listen, I've got something to ask you, and I want you to promise you'll tell me the truth.'

'OK.'

'Is he gay?'

'Is who gay?'

'Jack.'

'Jack? No!' It was the first time I'd smiled all week.

'Are you sure you're telling me the truth?'

'Yes, Mum.'

'Because I've heard that all the gays go to San Francisco, is that right?'

'Well, some of them do. But Jack's not one of them.'

'All right, darling, if you say so. I can't imagine why else he'd leave. You said he wasn't cheating on you.'

'No.'

'Mother worries about you, you know.'

'I know.'

'I won't keep you, then. Goodbye, darling, I love you.'

'I love you too.'

'Age: 36. Occupation: Artist. Weight: 160 lbs. Height: 5'11".' The ad seemed all right so I agreed to a date. He might have been five-eleven, if he'd ever stood up straight; as it was, I'll never know. While he explained how open-minded he was, I bought him a drink.

162

'*You*'re buying *me* a drink?' he exclaimed. To cut a long mono- logue short, he was a graphic designer. This was how I worked it out.

'So,' I posited, 'you get money for computer-based visual art- works, and they have a commercial element?'

'Yes.'

'So you're a graphic designer.'

'Well . . . I mean, that's my *job*, I suppose. So you could say that . . . if that's how you like to think about things.' Then he pontificated on his scrap sculptures, his artistic vision and his ideas for the future of society. 'I don't like grown-ups. There's something so . . . limited about them, you know?'

'Mmm,' I remarked.

In his case, rejecting the standard indices of adulthood seemed to boil down to not buying a house, but I'm all for home-ownership, especially in prospective husbands. An hour later, it was over – I had promised to go to the Odious to see Mr Twinkles, private detective by day, lounge singer by night. The Artist insisted on driving me there on his motorbike, thus obliging me to hitch my skirt up to my knickers. When I wriggled back on to *terra firma* and pulled my skirt back down, he took my hand and said, 'I'd like to see you again,' before revving back into obscurity. These men must have been consulting the same dating manual.

Listening to Mr Twinkles croon about love, my mood blackened. I'd been just as nervous about that date as the last one – I had *laboured* over my outfit, *fretted* over where to meet, *agonized* over how to describe my vacuum of a life, and *fantasized* over what he might be like. All a complete waste of time and effort because there was nobody for me, anywhere. Nobody! Anywhere! Linda, I told myself, you should have a fucking lobotomy and then they'd seem a lot more interesting.

Heidi arrived and I followed her to the bar where I gazed deject- edly into my beer. A couple came over to say they loved Cotton

Candy, but their sweet words didn't help. Why had I ever left the house? I should have stayed in and read a book, got to grips with string theory. A god-like blond guy drifted past, like a character from a dream, or a 1970s sex movie set on a beach. There are people in the world like that, I thought, glaring at the dregs in my glass, but I don't get to meet them. I get to meet the one I met tonight and it's all because of fucking Fate . . .

'I like your hair!'

The blond god's beautiful face was split in two by an outsize smile.

We got talking. His name was Sven. Since moving to the city six months back, he'd spent his nights working on an animated film; he also made sculptures, wrote songs, sang, played cello and piano and knew what a key signature was. I got his email address on the pretext of inviting him to our gig on Monday, and spent the weekend in a flap. What if he came? What if he didn't?

He didn't. But the electronic courtship dance had begun, and little did I know that the slow pace of things would be enough to turn me into a rabid succubus. He asked all the right questions, except 'Would you like to meet up?' When I invited him to a party, he said he was going snowboarding[16] and made no return invitation.

Three tormented weeks passed until Heidi talked me down over the phone, like air-traffic control: 'Don't give up now, Lindy-loo. Don't give up. Just ask him one more time.'

16 A stroke of luck, as it turned out to be a panties party, to which the Fat Magician wore a leather thong.

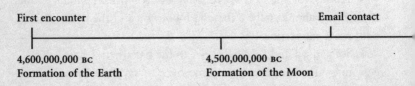

First encounter		Email contact
4,600,000,000 BC	4,500,000,000 BC	
Formation of the Earth	Formation of the Moon	

'What's the point? It's hopeless, like everything else!'

'Please!'

'Why?'

'Because I asked you to. Go on – one more time. Do it for me.'

'I can't.'

'One more time.'

I invited him to come along with my friends to see a 'great band' and, to my amazement, he agreed. Now all I had to do was find some friends and a band.

Like the executioner's blade, Saturday night fell all too soon. As we awaited his arrival, I stood in the corner of a dark bar, huddling penguin-style into my friends. His age was the burning question – clearly it was low, but how low would I go? Online stalking told me he'd graduated in 2000, so he could be twenty-six, if he was a slow learner. I grasped Tom's sleeve. 'What if he's only twenty-four?'

'Then I'd say good on you!' He snickered. 'What if he brings a date?'

Heidi told him to shut up.

After twenty minutes, I entered adrenalin after-shock and slumped. 'He's not coming.'

'He'll come, Pumpkin.'

'No . . . we should go. He's not coming.'

'Sure he is,' said Heidi. 'There he is now.'

A blond head was bobbing above the crowd. I made a break for the bar, then escaped to the loo, where I stared at my panicked face in the mirror before forcing myself back into the fray. Soon it was time to leave for the 'great band': a heavy metal act consisting of

First group date

4,200,000,000 BC
First life on Earth

one man and five robots. I thought it might have novelty value. Heidi said, 'I'm gonna find out how old he is,' and marched off while I studied the knots in the table-top. Then she was back, breathing in my ear: 'He's twenty-three.' She patted my arm, grinning. 'He thought we were twenty-two.'

Tom sidled up. 'Talk to him!'

I tried, but there seemed to be some kind of force-field . . .

Heidi dragged me back to his side, saying, 'Sven's into sewing, Lindy-loo. He's making himself a fur coat out of wool!' She elbowed me.

'Oh, wow!' I said. 'Um, what's the wool like?'

'Well, it's dark brown, and I'm making it in these looped sections . . .'

The band was dreadful, and my loyal supporters quickly peeled off, forcing me to speak to the special guest. By midnight, it was just the two of us, driving round my neighbourhood. One of us was drunk.

'Hotter,' I said, as we turned another corner.

'Hotter . . . colder . . . much colder . . . bit hotter . . .'

'Warm . . . warmer . . .'

At last I conceded that he'd found my house. The moment we drew to a halt, I was catapulted from the car by nervous energy – ''Bye!' I yelled, as I flew through the night.

Inside my house, I noticed it was strangely hard to walk, and saw that my shoes were on the wrong feet.

Tim burst into my room the next morning. 'So, did you snog him?'

First time alone together

3,800,000,000 BC
Earth's crust solidifies

Then Tom rang. 'Did you get laid, Pumpkin? . . . What do you mean, no? You made out, though, right?'

'No.'

'After we put in all that effort? Oh, Lord.'

Heidi called. 'Did you make out? . . . Why not?'

I tried to explain that it was the embarrassment of facing somebody new, who was bound to have more experience than me, and I assured her I was over my jitters, and I'd do better next time.

And I had a ruse: as Cinderella had left her glass slipper at the ball, I had left my ear-muffs in Sven's car. I asked him to bring them to the International Women's Day celebrations, where Cotton Candy was playing, but regretted the invitation the moment I found myself singing about anal sex beneath a giant, pink, neon vagina.

'It's OK!' said Tom. 'It's good he knows what he's getting into. Or, rather, not.'

My date approached the stage, offering the muffs like a blue acrylic olive branch. 'Thanks!' I said, grabbing them *en route* to the dressing room. Luckily, Tom waylaid him at the exit while Heidi gave me a pep-talk.

'Lindy-loo, you're not doing too well on the old chit-chat. Come on now – go outside and talk to him.'

I stepped out with clenched fists, and stood next to him, but the only sound I could make was a high-pitched hum. 'Stage nerves!' explained Tom.

'I guess I should be going now,' said Sven, padding sadly to his car.

'Thanks for coming!' I called thinly, as he drove off. Too little, too late.

Second date

1,500,000,000 BC
First multi-cellular organisms

Tom chuckled. 'Pumpkin, a month from now you'll be lying in bed together, laughing about this. Trust me! Look in your bag.'

I looked.

'Is he in there?'

'No.'

'He's in there. Trust me, honey – men are easy.'

Encouraged by Tom, I sent an apologetic note with the daring suggestion that we meet *sans* chaperones. He agreed, but turned up with one of his own – Andy, a friend from LA who was up for the weekend. Ostensibly in search of a café, I led us through North Beach, across Fisherman's Wharf, past the Golden Gate Bridge and up the cliffs – on and on through the brilliant day until, three hours later, I petered out at a bus stop and curled into a low-sugar ball, all nervous energy spent.

Jack still used my address as he wasn't of entirely fixed abode. Every other Tuesday he came over to pick up his unemployment cheque and have a sad little conversation with me. In the interests of fairness, I filled him in on my romantic endeavours.

'So, have you met anyone else yet, Lins?'

'Well, sort of.'

'That's great!'

His cheeriness on this subject always hurt me. 'It's not going to happen,' I said despondently.

'Why not?'

'He's twenty-three.'

'You never know, Lins. What's he like?'

Third date

500,000,000 BC
First vertebrates (fish)

168

'Really sweet, shy, sincere, charming, beautiful, blond, blue-eyed, six-four, really strong, lifts weights, runs, works for the Star Wars company, plays the piano really well, and the cello, and the guitar, and sings, and makes giant sculptures. He's completely adorable and he has a car.'

Jack took a reflective puff on his cigarette. 'Lins, can I ask you something?'

'What?'

'Have you slept with him yet?'

'Why do you want to bring it down to that?'

'I don't know. Just, have you?'

I took a deep breath. 'Not yet.'

Sven finally suggested we meet up, this time for tea in the park.

'Tom, he wants to meet up for fucking tea in broad daylight! What does that say to you?'

'Well, honey, I'd say he wants to have some tea with you.'

Would you . . . ?

Would you like to join me for a cup of tea?
We could have ourselves a pleasant little chat.
You may find that I'm as right for you as you for me!
But then things don't tend to work out quite like that . . .

I'm dying to ask you, but I can't get near.
It's just that I don't want you to get the right idea.

Fourth date discussed

430,000,000 BC
Waxy-coated algae begin to live on land

Would you like to join me for a little walk?
Then I wouldn't have to look into your eyes.
Maybe I would stumble and your arms would break my fall!
But it's such a waste of time to fantasize . . .

I'm dying to ask you, but I can't get near.
It's just that I don't want you to get the right idea.

Would you care to join me and a dozen friends
For a super-casual evening in a bar?
They're only there as cover so that I can talk to you
'Cause perhaps a one-on-one is going too far.

I'm dying to ask you, but I can't get near.
It's just that I don't want you to get the right idea . . .

He chuckled. 'Don't worry, Pumpkin, he's in the bag.'

'But I don't want to have a stupid cup of tea with him. I can't stand being polite any more. Do you know what our conversations are like? I'm, like, "Stones are great, aren't they?" and he's, "Yeah. That's something I really like about you. You like stones." "And bricks. I lived in a house made of bricks." "Yeah, bricks. Bricks are good too. Yup . . . That's something else I really like about you. You've lived in houses made of interesting materials." "And then there's wood!" "Yup. Wood's very nice. Like you; you're very nice." "Thank you. And don't forget clapboard."'

'Honey, just say you wanna get laid!'

I hung up on Tom and changed the date to dinner and a robot show: I was determined to get some decisive action.

But first came Valentine's Day, and one person never forgot me:

Dear Linda
This is just a little note to tell you that I love you and want
more than anything for you to be happy. Happiness doesn't
always just arrive, though, and might at times seem elusive, but
I'm sure you can find it if you continue to search for it. Just
remember, little things can make you happy too. Have a good
Valentine's Day. Lots and lots of love, Mum
XXXXXXXXXXXXXXXXXXXXXXXXXX

The next day was Friday, and Jack turned twenty-seven. He was tiring of the whole drugs-and-trying-to-have-sex lifestyle and had a nasty cold to boot, so I made him dinner while he snuffled by the TV, moaning. 'Oh, Lins,' he said, 'I'll never have kids.'

'Jack, you're so melodramatic.'

'It's a tragedy, really.'

'Why are you saying all this?'

'Because . . . you know. I can't get a stiffy, can I? Ironic, isn't it, how I want to leave you to have sex with other women, and now I can't have sex with anyone at all?'

'Hmm.' I smiled at the wall.

'I can't feel my toes after a few minutes if I sit down . . .'

At ten, I left him to his misery.

The next day was Saturday, and Sven came over for dinner. I was

Fourth date

230,000,000 BC
Cockroaches and termites evolve

so excited my stomach was knotted. He seemed to have difficulty swallowing, and keeping the conversation afloat was like rowing with chopsticks. It was a relief when we drove off into a torrential thunderstorm and sat through an hour of loud bangs and flashes of light in a warehouse down by the docks, where machines made of junk spat fire and spun people round. I won a balloon.

Afterwards, we walked distractedly for a mile or so, uphill in the rain, until we got to my favourite cocktail bar. After a couple of vodkas, Sven began to talk: '. . . that's something I really like about you . . . I like English accents . . . that's another thing I really like about you . . . I like your pink and fuzzy sweater . . . your hair's a good colour, not too neon . . . I really like that about you.'

He went to the loo, and came back with his hair realigned. 'You're so positive and optimistic – that's another thing I really like about you.'

I smiled and changed the subject. 'So what's your family like?'

His perfectly moulded cheeks reddened slightly, and he looked at his feet. 'My family is . . .'

This sounded serious. 'They're what?'

'They're very – um . . . religious.'

'So?'

'I thought you wouldn't like me if you knew.'

'Well, my family's really sad – do you like me less now?'

'No.'

'Well, then.'

Such things prove so important in the end, yet they never seem that way when you're sitting in a bar.

200,000,000 BC
Pangaea starts to break apart

172

We set off down the hill like a pair of tightening springs, and with each step his praise became more lavish: 'I'd like to speak with your mum, Linda. I'd thank her for having such a nice daughter.' But when we got to my gate, he just stood there in his cream coat, like a slab of vanilla ice-cream. Yet again it was up to me. 'Soooo . . .' I said, intent on getting the words out before I drowned in adrenalin '. . . um, I have to ask, it's kind of, well, am I going to – going to get to kiss you or do you just want to be friends?'

The outsize smile lit up. 'We will . . . definitely get to kiss each other.'

Noting the future tense, I gave up for the night, and bade him goodnight as the gate slammed behind me.

'Goodnight!'

Next, I offered to cut his hair – perhaps some intimate touching might spur him into action. As there was a bed in his bedroom, we sat in the lounge, amid a haze of tension. He said he was entering his film in a festival, and I said, 'That's great.' I sliced my finger at first snip, but at last it was done and we went out for dinner, where I downed a bit of lettuce while he said more things he liked about me before we drove off again. 'You seem to be going towards my house,' I noted.

'Um, yes.'

'Are you intending to drop me off?'

'Um, is there . . . any alternative?'

And there we were, outside my house, both staring at the dashboard. 'So,' I said, 'what's going on?'

Fifth date

145,000,000 BC
Archaeopteryx walks the earth

'If you mean, "Are we in a relationship?" then, yes, we are.'

'Right . . .'

'It's just maybe, er, I dunno, things are moving a bit fast for me.'

'Things' were moving about as fast as the car. 'Fast? Sven, there's slow, and then there's static. *This* is static.'

There was a sticky pause. 'It's just,' he stammered, 'it's been a long time since I've had a . . . a serious relationship.'

'And?'

He sighed as if I'd ordered him to clean out the fridge, and asked if he could kiss me.

I said yes, 'but not in this ugly car'. Nervous but determined, I led him to my bedroom where, in response to his unresponsiveness, I grabbed his arm and dived underneath it. Still no kiss. With his free arm, he began to play a soothing one-handed tune on the melodica. I asked him why he was so useless.

'I couldn't believe that someone like you, you know . . . I guess I was a bit intimidated. I guess . . . you stand for everything I think is cool.'

I would have been less surprised if he'd thought I was an Eskimo. At dawn, still unkissed, I followed him to the front door and pressed my lips upon his.

'I know,' he said. 'I was going to . . .'

Things went on like this for a while. When he came round to play, we'd perch at opposite ends of the sofa for half an hour and talk stiffly until I made a move. I complained about this and he started sitting on top of me, but still didn't take off his clothes – or mine. Six weeks in, and I hadn't seen my new boyfriend's chest.

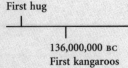

First hug

136,000,000 BC
First kangaroos

174

'Sven,' I said, as we lay in each other's fully clothed arms, 'do you want to be a grandfather?'

'Well, yes, one day, I suppose.'

'So first you'll need to be a father.'

'Mm-hmm . . . ?'

'So, at some point, you're probably going to have to take your shirt off in front of a woman.'

A snail would have been tapping its foot with impatience.

First kiss

65,000,000 BC
Extinction of dinosaurs

10: Getting It – Finally

> *'Things will turn your way in the end, my darling.*
> *You just keep trying.'*
>
> *Mum*

When Jack came round to pick up his unemployment cheque, he asked, 'How's it going with the kid?'

'Kid?'

'That boy.'

He always asked, and I always fobbed him off: the best way to milk this was to keep him in the dark, as his imagination couldn't fail to outstrip the reality.

'It's great that you've found someone, Lins. I'm really pleased for you.'

'Thanks,' I said, my fists scrunched into hammers.

'So . . . is he a good kisser?'

'Yes . . . Look, Jack, let's not talk about it.'

'Better than me?'

'Please! Anyway, you're not telling me *your* business any more, are you?'

Stays the night: no sex

50,000,000 BC
First monkeys

4,000,000 BC
Hominid bipedalism

'Oh, yes. I've had some escapades, all right.' He laughed mirth-lessly.

'Like what?'

'That's different, Lins.'

'Why?'

'It just is.'

'Why won't you tell me? You must want to, or you wouldn't have mentioned it.'

'No, Bun, I can't tell you. I just can't.'

I assumed he was trying to protect me, but I was wrong – for some reason, he was *ashamed*: 'I can't tell anyone. If the girls at home knew, they'd never let me live it down.'

There was no way I was letting this go. 'Come on,' I said, 'you can tell *me*.'

'No, I can't.'

'Please?'

He thought for a moment. 'I mean, if I did you've got to swear you'll never tell anyone, Lins. Not ever, not a soul.'

'OK, I promise.'

'No, I mean it, you've got to promise and really mean it.'

'I promise.'

'It's so embarrassing. I mean, it's really funny, but it's awful.'

'Just tell me!'

'OK, well, do you swear? I mean it. Do you swear?'

'Yes.'

'You won't tell anyone?'

'No.'

Takes T-shirt off, unprompted		Takes my T-shirt off, prompted

2,000,000 BC
Stone tools invented

'OK. Well, it's like this . . .'

And he proceeded to tell me a story that I cannot share with another living soul. I must insist therefore that you refrain from reading the following song, which you can hear on the Cotton Candy album *Poppycock!* available at cdbaby.com and participating record stores.

The Arsehole

He met her after midnight, and she took him home,
He thrust her to the mattress, she began to moan,
'Hold me, love me, break me, kiss me deep and long!'
Tiny prickles brushed his hand, but he just carried on.

Oh, how was he to know? How was he to know?
He was too inexperienced to just say no.

He tore her satin bra off; two boobs hit the floor.
Her panties were protruding, big surprise in store,
But an arsehole is an arsehole, on woman or on man,
So he flipped her over and the dirty work began.

Oh, how was he to know? How was he to know?
He was too inexperienced to just say no.

Afterwards they lay there, bodies drenched in sweat,
The scene was set for romance, sheets tangled and wet.

Takes my T-shirt off, unprompted

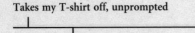

1,600,000 BC
Homo erectus

Then he saw the chest hair, smelt the manly smell,
Horror filled his lonely heart, 'Please don't ever tell!'

Oh, how was he to know? How was he to know?
He was too inexperienced to just say no.

Now it's really no big deal to swing the other way,
But he was so embarrassed at being accidentally gay
That he never told a soul, till I sat upon his knee, whisp'ring,
'Don't you worry, Jack, for your secret's safe with me . . .'

I wasn't buying it. 'Don't tell me you didn't notice! You must've twigged before you got into bed.'

'Well, no, she was really tiny – I mean he – and really pretty, and he had loads of makeup on. It was really dark, too.'

'Didn't he say anything?'

'I suppose, yes, in the taxi, he said, 'So, do you like boys as well as girls?' I guess I kind of realized then, but I didn't want to think about it.'

'Jack!'

'Yeah . . .' He giggled. 'I met him in the street yesterday, just by chance. I didn't recognize him, coz he was in jeans. He came up to me and said, 'Hello, my beautiful British boy!' God, it was so embarrassing. Lins, you really can't tell this to anyone . . .'

While Jack's love life became more and more colourful, Sven's sexual reticence would have tried the patience of a saint. I asked him what

Genital touching: mutual

1,000,000 BC
First use of fire

he used to get up to on 'dates'. 'Well,' he replied, 'we'd meet up, have some tea and, you know, see what happened.' Not much, it turned out – he'd kissed only two of his datees.

'Would the others have known they were dating you?'

'Probably not.'

'Um,' he said, nervously, 'I have a sort of secret.'

'Go on,' I said, but I already knew what it was. I wrapped my arms round him from behind, to hide my face while my heart sank: I'd got myself another bloody virgin.

My two virgins came face to face at the next Cotton Candy show. Sven was in high spirits because his film had won an award at the festival, and though I was anxious about the meeting, I was in raptures over him – he was soft and gentle, like good toilet paper, and ridiculously attractive. I felt like I'd gone shopping for a second-hand Volkswagen and come home with a sparkling new Porsche. Jack had been enthusiastic about meeting 'the kid', but the moment he saw him, his face fell. 'Wow,' he said. 'He's *really* good-looking, Lins.'

'Yup,' I said, my triumph sullied by guilt.

'He looks like a lovely kid. Much better than me.'

'Mmm. Do you want to talk to him?'

'No, not tonight. It's too much, all at once.'

'OK.' I nodded.

He turned to go, then grabbed my arm. 'Excuse my asking, Lins, but, um, have you done it yet?'

'Done what?'

'You know. With that kid.'

'Can we not talk about it, please?'

Shared bath   Genital touching, unprompted

200,000 BC
Neanderthal man

180

'Why not?'

'Because I don't want to.'

'You don't want to sleep with him?'

'No, I don't want to talk about it.'

'I'm sorry, Lins, it's just, I really want to know. I don't know why.'

'I'm going to get a drink.'

'So have you?'

I went to the bar, and Tom came over to join me. He gestured at Sven. 'So, have you two done it yet, Pumpkin?'

'. . . No.'

'What? When are you gonna get some action, Pumpkin?'

'Ssh! Look, Tom, I'm getting some "action", OK?'

'A little dry humping? That doesn't count.'

Heidi came over and shook her head. 'Lindy-loo, it's been weeks! I can't believe you still haven't done it!'

Sensing my tension, Sven came up and held my hand.

At home, it was the same story. Tina put down her bagel in disbelief. 'You haven't done it yet? Why not?'

'Oh, you know, I don't want to push it.'

'Wouldn't it be funny if it turns out he was a virgin this whole time?'

'Mmm.'

All this time, Sven had a single bed; when he bought a double, I went over to help test it. After about two hours of fooling around, I took charge of the situation once and for all, and suggested we actually do it. You know, *it*. I knew I wouldn't have long, but I'd delayed orgasm for about three months by this point and, amazingly,

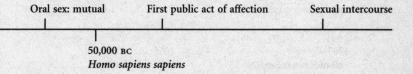

Oral sex: mutual   First public act of affection   Sexual intercourse

50,000 BC
Homo sapiens sapiens

181

it was a tie. (And, it turned out, he was a gentleman as he used his elbows.)

'Shouldn't we have . . . ?'

'No, I told you. It's sorted.' I had a little device that flashed red or green lights.

Seeing that I had a new stud saddled up, Jack felt able to burden me with his woes, and broke down every time we met, leaving a trail of tears and drool down the front of his T-shirt. 'I'll never find anybody as sweet as you, Linda, because there *is* nobody as sweet as you.'

I put my cat down and looked at him in surprise.

'God,' he mused, 'thinking about how this feels for me, I can't imagine how horrible what I did must have been for you.'

'Mmm.' The longed-for vindication fell flat.

'Excuse me for asking,' he continued, 'but have you slept with him yet?'

I turned to face him, arms crossed. 'Why do you always ask that?'

'I dunno . . .'

Suddenly he burst into tears. 'I just hate my mum,' he sobbed. 'Silly bitch – I hate her for having me. I hate her! And now I have to stay alive for her!' He adored his mum, and with good reason, but right now I was the only person he had to confide in.

The next time we met he had a terrible cut down his arm. 'I almost fell down three flights of stairs at the weekend, I was so pissed, but luckily I managed to grab hold of the railing.' I bit my lip, imagining the potential hospital bill. He already owed money everywhere. By moving furniture a couple of days a week, and

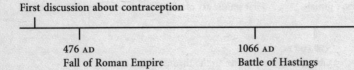

First discussion about contraception

476 AD
Fall of Roman Empire

1066 AD
Battle of Hastings

182

flogging overpriced candy at night, he was making about $600 a month over his rent, which wasn't nearly enough to cover his expenses:

1. cocktails for himself and the girls he wanted to sleep with
2. cigarettes
3. dope
4. ecstasy
5. speed
6. heroin[17]

When the time came to eat, he'd borrow money, oozing repentance and self-loathing, but as he had no memory for numbers he was always genuinely shocked when I asked for it back. I had to be a bitch to get it but, as he had so often pointed out, I was good at that. One day, he called with a business-like tone: 'Hi, Lins, Jack here. Listen, I'm moving into a shelter. Do you think I could leave my stuff in your room?'

'What kind of shelter? Like, for homeless people?'

'Yes.'

'You're not homeless, Jack.'

'I can't pay rent.'

'You can't move into a shelter. You won't like it.'

'What else can I do? I'm desperate, I'm a mess, I can't pay for

17 Thankfully that only went on for a few weeks, or this would be an obituary and I'd have to be nice.

1558 AD
Queen Elizabeth I comes to the throne

anything else ... I can't stay here ... I haven't got any money for food and by the time I get my next unemployment cheque I'll be two months behind on the rent ...'

I told him off, sorted something with Mum and paid his back rent on condition that he would stay put.

'Thanks so much, Lins.'

'It's a loan.'

Then I met someone he'd slept with. It was our first Cotton Candy show with our newest member, Matt, a marvellous malleting marimba player who brought in hundreds of extra notes. He wasn't an alcoholic, just a keen drinker with all kinds of musical curlicues up his frilly sleeves. We were performing at the Folsom Street Fair, San Francisco's annual S&M Mecca, and the perverts were out in force. Tom scratched his head in wonder. 'Why on earth did they book us?'

I shrugged. 'Our songs are quite rude, I suppose.'

'But we're not black, leathery and covered with cum.'

'Speak for yourself,' piped up Matt, mallets to the fore.

Heidi was squeezed into a pink rubber mini-dress.

'For our first number, we'd like to do a love song ...'

After the set, a professional bondage clown called Scratchy told her she was really 'hot!' She completely lost it, spitting venom at the rubber guys 'n' dolls cavorting on all sides. 'Lindy-loo! How come all the guys who like me are big, fat, disgusting CLOWNS?' Someone pointed his camera at her bottom and she turned on him: 'If you wanna take a picture of my ass, ask me first!' Then, all at once, tantrum forgotten, she grabbed my arm and pointed across the room. 'Oh, my God! That's *her*, Lindy-loo!'

More sexual intercourse (missionary)

1789 AD
French Revolution

184

'Who?'

'Ms Potatohead – the one Jack slept with at Christmas with the ginormous ass!'

'Where?'

'Over there, dancing. She's got a *huge* ass!'

She did. I walked over, tapped her arm and said brightly, 'You slept with my husband!'

'Er,' she stuttered, 'no, I didn't!'

'Yes, you did!' smiled Heidi, reassuringly. 'You remember – Jack, tall British guy, dark, kinda handsome . . .'

'Oh, yeah . . .' Ms Potatohead looked nervously at me.

'Oh, Lindy-loo doesn't mind,' said Heidi.

I nodded. 'He needed the practice.'

She relaxed. 'Yeah, he was nice. We made out, but I don't sleep with people I don't know.'

I shook my head. 'Course not.'

Thank goodness for Mum.

Dear Linda

It was nice to hear your voice on the phone last night. When you phone you must get into the habit of asking if Dad's in and then you'll know that I can't say all that I'd like to, e.g. that I put another £200 into your account yesterday. I did that merely to keep you out of debt. I'm looking forward to having a leisurely chat with you when we're together again, without the pressure of being on the phone and time running out. Please

1939 AD
Second World War begins

use the extra cash sensibly – a new violin case? I do love you,
my darling, Mum XXXXX

I got a red light but I was prepared. Lured by the promise of 'unbelievable sensation', I'd spent some of Mum's money on Natural Lamb condoms, made from real sheep, but when Sven ripped open a glossy sachet, out fell a shrivelled pink snakeskin, covered with slime, which made me shriek. I tossed this sorry specimen across the room, and we were still laughing when Tina's horrid cat opened the door, sniffed, picked up the condom and ate it. This was a good start to Sven's birthday. The treats continued with a twenty-four-candle cupcake and a T-shirt on which I'd written NICE in rhinestones. We spent the afternoon wading through kids in the museum, looking at skulls, and when we got back, his phone rang. He took the call in the next room and came back looking troubled. 'It was my mom. I told her about the skulls, and she asked who I went with, so I said, "My girlfriend," and there was this silence. Then she started going on about young women who just want to get pregnant to trap a man.'

'Why was she so surprised?'

'Oh. Um. You know when I told you that I'd talked to her about you?'

'Yes.'

'I was lying.'

And so began his mother's campaign of terror, waged from the depths of rural Minnesota. She didn't know I was married; it was enough that I wasn't Christian. I wondered how his elder siblings had dealt with it. 'Oh,' he said, 'they're good Christians. They both

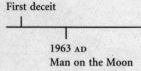

First deceit

1963 AD
Man on the Moon

186

still live in my parents' town. My sister lives up the road, and my brother lives in the basement.'

'Have they ever dated anyone?'

'No, not as far as I know.'

My own mother also had an agenda.

'Is there any chance, Linda? Has he said anything?'

'Listen, Mum, I'm not going to get back together with Jack.'

'Oh, darling, it's just . . .'

'What?'

'Well, it didn't last long, did it?'

'We were together for six and a half years, Mum. Listen, I've got something to tell you and you might be pleased and you might be angry.'

'Go on.'

'I've got a new boyfriend.'

The Atlantic heaved between us.

At last, she spoke. 'I'm pleased.'

Unleashed, I raved about his height, job, car and piano-playing ability in that order.

'Well, darling,' she concluded, 'let's hope it turns into something.'

'It *is* something. Mum, I've just told you it's something.'

'Well, we'll see, darling.'

I hung up, infuriated. It *was* something. Wasn't it?

2008 AD
What Rhymes with Bastard? published

Part Three: *More Endings*

11: My Name Is Linda and I Am a Failure

'Look at your bedroom – it's such a mess! Linda, no one'll ever marry you!'

Mum

Teaching the violin was a relatively painless way to collect money, but I couldn't find enough students to cover my rent. I had to target the beginners, and the drop-out rate was about 90 per cent. Everyone seemed to think I could be doing 'something better', but no one knew what it was. I carried on sending out copywriting CVs, desultorily applied for some basic office jobs, got rejected from a pub kitchen because I wouldn't touch eggs, failed the entrance exam to be a salesperson in a bookshop, and then I gave up.

I felt good when I was with Sven, but was flailing quietly otherwise, so I turned to the free clinic for help. To my surprise, they didn't mind that I wasn't a tramp or a drug addict, and directed me to a lavatory-sized room where a gentle man asked me what the trouble was.

'Um, nothing really,' I said. 'I suppose I've come to a strange country where I don't know anyone . . .'

'Mmm . . . ?'

'. . . and I lost my career, which was shit anyway . . .'

'Uh-huh . . .'

'. . . and, yes, I guess my education was a complete waste of time . . . I've never tried hard at anything so now I'll never have anything, and I have no money and my husband left me because he wanted to sleep with other people and he told me all about it and I think I'm a loser and I don't believe in my creative projects and my mum tells everyone I'm happily married with a great job and unless I'm with my boyfriend I want to cry and I can't tell him I'm sad.'

He signed me up for long-term therapy. No charge.

When Jack came to pick up his next cheque, he was all smiles. 'Listen, Lins,' he said, 'I've *met* someone!'

'That's great!'

'I hope you don't mind me telling you this.'

'Absolutely not.'

I didn't. I felt nothing but relief. He'd been working as a Peachy Puff boy, selling sweets at a Yes show, when Matoko, twenty-five, had taken a shine to his lollipops. Half Japanese, all American and visiting from Indiana, she'd recently got married without telling her parents, then had an abortion without telling her husband, who had gone insane and disappeared, prompting her to drop out of college for the fourth time and move back in with her evil, ailing mother, on whom she waited hand and foot, only to be repaid with cruelty and abuse. 'Yeah,' grinned Jack, 'I've found someone as desperate as me.'

Two days later he called to tell me he was moving to Indiana with Matoko. 'It's ridiculous, I know, but I'm killing myself out here. I've got to make a change, whatever it is.'

'What are you going to do there?'

'I dunno, flip burgers or something. I'm excited, but it's so last-minute. We'll see how long it lasts. Not even half my stuff'll fit in the car. I'll miss you so much, Bun.'

'Mmm,' I said. 'Can I have the Le Creuset casserole dish?'

I got the portable stereo, too. An excellent outcome.

I wasn't sorry to see him go because I had Sven. The pair of us spent the next evening curled up before his favourite movie, a saccharine romp about a prince who abandons his beloved to seek his fortune. I was glad when it ended and we rolled into bed, but when I turned off the light, he started talking about his work, and how he needed to make a decision soon, and this and that and so on and so forth, and he was leaving town to seek his fortune. You know, probably.

'You're what?'

'Well, maybe. I mean I haven't . . . I don't . . . Who knows?'

In the wake of the animation festival, he'd been headhunted within an inch of his life. With his career goals suddenly realizable, he had seen that he didn't want them after all. No, he was going to ditch his job, move back to his college town, live off his savings and develop some amazing new graphics software that would make him a billionaire by the year 2015. In his spare time, he would make chairs. The college town offered old friends, cheap rent and good cheese; San Francisco had nothing but hills and me, and I was getting a bit scary: if things carried on like this, he might have to tell me he loved me, or at least give me a present.

'Well,' I said numbly, 'it'll be good for you to go out with someone else.'

'Huh?'

'I think you'll find you're a lot less shy when you get back there.'

'Huh?'

'Well, when you said you hadn't been with anyone else, I knew it had to end at some point.'

'Um . . . that couldn't have been very nice for you.'

'No.'

'I hadn't thought about going out with someone else, Linda.'

'Well, what did you think would happen?'

'I hadn't really thought about it.'

'Why not?'

193

'It isn't exactly . . . a nice thing. I don't know, things have been so good between us in the past couple of months . . . maybe you've been really happy or something.'

It took me a moment to absorb this. 'I've been really sad, actually.'

'Oh. I'm sorry.'

'It's not your fault. Well, it is now.'

Cars roared up the hill, casting grids of light on the ceiling.

'With my last girlfriend, we had this unspoken agreement that we wouldn't contact each other when she left for school.'

'If it was unspoken,' I said, 'how do you know you agreed? Maybe she was really upset.'

'I hadn't thought of that.'

I was an idiot, dating a teenager.

'I really like you, Linda,' he added.

'Well, I more than "really like" you,' I replied. 'Do you ever want to feel more than that you "really like" someone?'

'. . . No . . . It's just the way I feel. I guess I'm not a very passionate person.'

I was an idiot, dating an emotional cripple, and I howled. At first light, I gathered my belongings from his room, tears dripping from my nose. The sniffing and commotion woke him up and he offered me a ride home.

'No,' I said, 'I'm trying to get away from you.'

I bawled on the bus and through the morning, afternoon and early evening, and then I went out to a birthday party with Heidi.

Sven threw up when I left, and concluded that he must love me after all. Nonetheless, he resigned from his job and booked a truck for three weeks hence. He tried to persuade me to stow away in the van, but good sense prevailed, and as he drove off to spend the next three years in a library with his computer, I was playing the violin for a wedding in City Hall. I hoped both couples would be very happy.

*

Dear Linda

I found a pad of these airmail letters in the bureau so I'm going to use them up; I can't imagine why I bought them originally. I keep thinking my pen's going to go right through the paper, so I'll write gently. I've been thinking about our phone conversation the other night. Darling, please take care of yourself and don't go alone to places at night if you can go with someone else, and keep to well-lit places, please. I do worry about you!! Yes, I'm nagging but only because I care about your safety.

Love, Mum XXX

The gentle man at the free clinic turned out to be a brilliant sage. Ten minutes into the session, he had unwittingly solved one of my biggest problems: I realized I wanted his job. As my career path crystallized, I sat in my chair and told him about all the great things I'd got out of my relationship with Sven. He nodded sympathetically.

'And can you tell me,' he asked, 'what you *didn't* get from this relationship?'

I gaped. He waited. Silence rose between us like water in a sinking cabin. I had to stop it. 'Well,' I blurted, 'I suppose he didn't tell me he loved me. And he wouldn't put Xs at the bottom of emails.'

He nodded. 'What else?'

More? The silence flooded in again. 'OK, OK. Um. He didn't give me any presents, which I didn't realize until the end. His life's full of cute reminders of me, like twisty plants and little blue pom-poms that sit on his desk, and a tiny apple, and a blue hat, and a silk eye mask coz he had to sleep in the day, and all kinds of little bats, the silly things you buy for loved ones . . .'

This man knew the importance of little bats. 'So,' he said, 'presents. What else?'

Come to think of it, there *were* quite a few things . . . 'Well, he'd be really late sometimes when I'd made him dinner, and only had enough time to eat it before he had to go to work, and I'd be crying before he turned up, but then I'd get all perky when he showed coz I didn't want him to think I was pathetic, so he never said sorry. And he didn't call me once for four days, and I was totally hysterical about it, and it turned out he'd been busy with his software project. I felt like I'd been put aside like a piece of knitting.'

'So, consideration for your feelings.'

'He wasn't mean, it just didn't occur to him.'

'We're not trying to assess whether he's at fault. Anything else?'

'And, um, emotional support, I suppose, but I get that from my friends. He wasn't really equipped to give great advice, so I guess that doesn't count.'

'It counts as something you didn't get. So, in many ways he didn't meet your needs.'

'They're not needs,' I objected, 'they're "wants".'

He nodded. 'OK. And if you don't get these "wants", what happens?'

'. . . I feel resentful.'

'Doesn't that make it a need?'

'Um. Yes.'

'Linda, I suggest you ask Sven to make a gesture that will make you feel valued.'

What?

Sven's gesture was to come back for my birthday, which we spent in bed with a bottle of vodka and a chocolate cake. On Monday morning, we'd got dressed again for the third time when the airport shuttle honked impatiently outside, half an hour early. Saying, 'I'm very sad to leave you, Linda,' he was whisked away, still tucking in his shirt.

After that, I felt disappointed every time I woke up – here I was again, another day spread before me like a wet picnic. I stopped calling him, and hid everything that brought him to mind.

196

Sad Song

I've packed away your photos in a box
And put them in a hard-to-reach place.
The book you gave me isn't on my shelf,
Instead there's just an empty space.

I've cleared out every bit and bob that makes me think of you.
I wish that I could reach inside and clear my head out too

The music that you gave me doesn't play now,
I've posted back the jacket you forgot,
Your sculpture is sitting in the cellar,
And that's the whole damned lot.

You're two thousand miles away, in a world of your own,
We're no longer even talking, yet you won't leave me alone.

Meanwhile Jack was on top form. His erectile dysfunction had temporarily abated, and he was back in business. 'Guess what?' he gushed. 'I slept with Amanda!'

'That's nice for you.'

'Well, yeah, but she – well, basically she *raped* me.'

'What do you mean, she raped you? She's five foot two.'

'She was totally high on coke, and she'd been up all night, and she came into my room at about five a.m. and, well, leaped on me. She didn't even take her knickers off, just moved the gusset out of the way.' He paused. 'I feel sort of used.'

'Isn't it a bit awkward now?'

'No, actually. I thought she was being really casual about it but it turns out she doesn't remember a thing. So maybe she'll do it again! You know, I think I'm kind of falling for her . . .'

He rode over my feelings like a gaudy parade float.

*

Things were also looking up for Heidi. She'd finally assented to go on a date with the nice, friendly artist her friend had lined up. I called her two days later to see how it had gone, and it was still going. 'I tell you, Lindy-loo,' she whispered into the phone, 'I know it's kinda dumb to say this now, but I think this is the man I'm gonna marry and have kids with!'

She had used the rhythm method, but her timing was off and, three dates in, she got pregnant. Nauseous for ten weeks straight, she developed a near-phobic dislike of onions, which she could detect from a hundred yards. Unfortunately this coincided with a long-standing booking to play at a friend's wedding. Determined not to let them down, Heidi hauled herself out of bed, tumbled down her front steps, in tranny-thick makeup, fluorescent eyelashes and a huge neon-pink gown, falling into the back seat with a thud. I turned round. 'How're you doing?'

'Uuugh,' she groaned, head in hands. 'I feel like total shit. I wanna barf so bad . . .'

When we arrived at the hall, she staggered upstairs, snapping at all who stood in her path.

'Are you the band?' asked a lilac-clad usher, deliberating on whether to let us pass.

'*No*,' croaked our singer, stomping past her. 'I always dress like this at weddings!'

Soon the first guests were seeping up the stairs; we began to play as the room filled with gabbing mouths. 'Oh, my God,' cried Heidi, 'I can smell onions!' She didn't throw up, but if she had done, I doubt anyone would have noticed. When we were done, I couldn't hide in the loo as I had to play 'Hava Nagila' while the bride and groom were hoisted aloft in their chairs and jolted round the room, faster and faster as the music speeded up.

I got a taste of Heidi's misery when I next went to the hospital for my anti-depressants. Weaned on the NHS, I had a homing instinct for social services, but in America there was a catch: free drugs meant a Soviet-style, three-stage rigmarole over at least two visits, standing in line for up to six hours, ticket in hand, in a bleak, sunless space, filled with sick, angry, impoverished people. I was usually the only white person on this side of the bullet-proof glass – unless they grow up in dire poverty, most Americans don't imagine you can get anything for free; it's as unthinkable as taking the bus. Once a month I was obliged to stand in line with some of the most impatient patients on earth, who cursed and hollered and complained and fought. Once I heard a commotion at the counter and looked up to see Fucchi Devine, Heidi's transvestite friend, who wasn't just dressing the part.

'Ma'am,' said the blank face, 'without proper photo ID we can't give you the medication.'

'Look at me!' cried Fucchi. 'I have boobs, and I have hair on my chin! I'm a transsexual. Do you know what that means? It means I'm a Nice Person!'

The technician made no response.

'I'm a nice person, and I'm getting terribly distressed about not getting my hormones! I need my hormones! I need them now!'

Another time, the lady next in line regaled me with her story, which involved her being a former prostitute and heroin addict, struggling with AIDS, lung cancer, high blood pressure, diabetes and hepatitis C. She was forty and she'd already had two heart-attacks.

But on this particular occasion I was hit by a horrific stench – a sickly-sweet, cloying blend of crusted urine, vomit and rotting flesh. I gagged and looked around, trying to identify the source.

A wavering, male voice piped up behind me: 'It's a long wait in this place.'

I half turned to nod, and the stench intensified. 'Yeah,' I said, trying not to breathe, 'that's true.' He looked like Father Christmas in an anorak.

'I can hear that you have an English accent.'

I turned round again just long enough to say, 'Yeah!'

'I lived there in . . . Let me see now, was it 1956? I was a teacher because at that time . . . Nearest underground was Highbury and Islington; do you know it?'

I half turned again. 'Yup.'

'Yes, I remember, there was a whole bunch of us because in those days anyone could get a teaching job in England.'

'Uh-huh.' He must be crazy. Best just to agree. I looked to the front of the line – about twenty people still to go – and held my glove in front of my mouth, trying to breathe through it.

'You must excuse my fragrance, my dear.' Guilt had me in its grip, and turned me to face the old man, who continued, 'It's because they need to put a new bag on my leg. I come into Emergency to sleep but they don't always have time to fix it up. All I've got to show for myself is a collection of bumps on the head and these tags!'

Around his wrist were a dozen orange bands from the emergency room. Steeling myself, I let him tell me about his degree and how his father had been leader of the Oakland Symphony and so on, and decided he was speaking the truth, which seemed even more tragic than his being crazy. At last, on the point of throwing up, I was called to the bullet-proof glass, but the pharmacist had bungled it and I had twenty more minutes to wait. Santa limped over. 'So lovely to talk to you,' he said.

'Oh,' I smiled, 'and you too.'

'Would you have some time to join me in the café, my dear?'

'Oh, no, I'm afraid I have to go.'

'You're in a rush?'

'Yes, I'm afraid so.' I was clearly not going anywhere.

'Are you sure?'

I was quite sure. To demonstrate how much of a rush I was in, I hid from him in the loo where I broke down in tears and missed them calling my name.

When I emerged, he was waiting for me, rheumy eyes full of hope. 'Just a few minutes?'

My gentle doctor had advised me to honour my 'authentic experience', which involved allowing my tears to flow and proved quite time-consuming. Crazy, Heidi's friendly friend with the lies, quickly christened me the Town Crier, and Heidi took me to task. 'Lindyloo,' she scolded, gently, 'you spent eighty per cent of your time together lying down – there's more to a relationship than nice cuddles. You've got to give it up!' Instead I spent fifty dollars and much of December knitting an embarrassingly elaborate mohair hat and scarf for my lost lover. The flatmates and I had a pirate-style Christmas with skull and crossbones, hats, eye-patches, and a treasure hunt at the beach, which would have been really fun if Sven had even sent me a card.

This disappointment triggered a migraine, during which a violin pupil arrived unexpectedly. I managed half an hour before I threw up into my hands. The spasm of vomiting lasted about thirty seconds, and all I had to aim for was an open-weave basket. 'Sorry,' I mumbled eventually. 'I guess you haven't had that reaction to your playing before.' She never came back. I did seem to be getting excessively upset over someone I'd known only for six months but, then, it wasn't really about him . . .

Off in the primitive wastelands of Indiana, Jack landed a job in a car factory. New environmental codes would soon be coming into force, raising production costs, and they were churning out as many toxic vehicles as possible to beat the deadline. He was living in a house surrounded by barking dogs, with a bisexual widow who fancied his girlfriend, Matoko. The house was so grim and the dogs so fierce he was glad to be out banging sheets of metal all day, except when the Christians asked if he was living in sin. When he'd gone to meet Matoko's family, they'd refused to speak to him because he was an adulterer. He'd then sent a letter of complaint to the sick mother, who'd responded by kicking Matoko out of the house. So he'd helped his shaking lovebird pack her bags and whisked her back to the dog-loving bisexual widow's place. I don't know why he told me all this, but it was very entertaining. Finally he asked how I was.

'I'm completely miserable, thank you for asking. That boy left when you did. He went to Wisconsin.'

'What? Oh, my God, I thought he was with you. I can't believe it. Why?'

'It's the cheese, I guess.'

'Lins, can I ask? Did you like him more than me?'

'Yes.'

'Can I ask why?'

Hmmm . . . gentler, kinder, prettier, sexier, happier, more lovable, more musical, more patient, more imaginative, better kisser, better cook, better dressed . . . 'I don't want to upset you, Jack.'

'Is it what I think it is?'

'What?'

'Does he have a bigger knob than me?'

12: Crazy for Love

> 'You don't want to jump into bed with the first person you meet.'
>
> Mum

Crazy turned twenty-six, and we went to the sauna to celebrate. I sat rather stiffly in the corner, with nothing to contribute.

Crazy: 'So, everyone, it's time for a change. I am now officially in search of true, long-lasting, for ever, babies-and-a-house Love. With a boy.'

Mitzi, the Adorable Nymphomaniac: 'A boy?'

Crazy: 'Definitely a boy.'

Mitzi: 'What about your power-bunny? Does that count as a boy?'

Crazy: 'No. It's pink and it can't talk.'

Heidi: 'What's the strangest crush you've ever had?'

Mitzi: 'I used to be in love with a statue. Have you ever French-kissed a statue? The stone dries your tongue out. It's not as hot as you'd think it'd be. Or as I thought it'd be. But, man, he was so buffed!'

Crazy: 'I used to make out with a statue of Jesus that was in my grandmother's front room.'

Mitzi: 'Did you ever leave any marks?'

Crazy: 'Oh, no, I don't think so ... I also made out with my computer screen and my TV. But that's normal – once I went into the yard and I found this girl I was living with making out with a post.'

Heidi: 'What kind of post?'

Crazy: 'A big wooden one. I mean, it didn't even have a face! That girl was a make-out fool . . .'

The party moves into the dry sauna.

Mini (another stripper friend of Heidi's): 'It's hard being a small girl with a Swedish man. Sometimes I just have to say to him, "Your whatnot ain't goin' in my coochee coz my coochee's broken! It's broken!"'

Mitzi: 'Oh, you shrink back to size. I handled porn-star proportions for four years . . .'

Mini: 'So I was getting this pain across my hip . . .'

Crazy: 'Sciatica.'

Mini: '. . . and I asked my mum how you get it, and she said, "Rough sex!"'

Heidi: 'Your mum said that?'

Mitzi: 'Yeah! Mini went with her mum to get her clitoris pierced.'

Pale English Girl (shocked): 'You took your mum?'

Mini: 'We got hers done, not mine!'

Heidi: 'Really? How old is she?'

Mini: 'Like, fifty.'

Heidi: 'So, was she cool about you being a stripper?'

Mini: 'Well, yeah, 'coz at my age she was a hooker. I'm not supposed to know. My dad told me.'

Crazy: 'How did he find out?'

Mini: 'Oh, he always knew. She bummed a cigarette off him. He was a valet-parking attendant, and she tried to . . . you know . . .'

Heidi sang 'Happy Birthday' to Crazy, lip-synching with her outsize labia. I was sitting next to her, so I missed the show; it seemed rude to bend over.

Afterwards the Adorable Nymphomaniac cooked us all dinner,

then exchanged her apron for a gold jacket and a transparent leopard-print G-string, stuck a candle between her butt-cheeks and bent over to sing 'Happy Birthday' to Crazy from between her legs. Her mating dance proved successful.

When Crazy suggested we move in together, I shut my eyes and leaped. Now that the helium-fuelled dot-com economy had collapsed, it was far easier to find an apartment, and we bagged a top-floor place in the Mission, the warmest part of town, where ragged palm trees sprang from the sidewalks. What joy to be warm again! We had an extra couple of rooms, and found two lovely girls to live in them: Sansa, a bondage-loving spiritualist who always wore orange, and Tyler, a bicycle-mad ex-fling of Crazy's, whom she'd dated at the same time as she dated Duckbill Pete: 'I told him, "It doesn't count if it's a girl."'

At first, Crazy seemed great to live with – tidy, paid bills, no live-in-lovers – but, strangely, she anticipated a bad ending. 'You know,' she said, 'people do seem to tire of me quickly. Every house I move into, something goes wrong and I have to leave and everything's horrid. That's not going to happen with us, is it?' I said I thought it was unlikely. She paid me incessant compliments, insisting I was the 'funnest person ever', and I couldn't resist. She began to dominate my social life, taking me out in outlandish costumes. She made me a pink lambskin dress with matching gauntlets, and slaved over an Astroturf corset. When she wasn't parading her wares at tame fetish events, we went swing-dancing, where she learned the man's part to ward off sweaty strangers. Her unusually high cortisol levels kept us on the hop – with absolutely no fear of strangers, she made everything exciting. She disguised me as a vampire in elaborate corsetry and black rubber, took me to a Goth club, told someone in a crow costume I fancied him, then drove me away in an old Volkswagen whose windscreen wipers never stopped, rain or shine.

She also put together a photo album with pictures of 'us', wanted to know my whereabouts at all times, and began to refer to me as her wife. I stayed home, writing, cooking and cleaning while she did the DIY and went out to work – a fair and equal partnership if I'd got half the cash. Familiar with obsessive, platonic love, I heard no alarm bells, happy to be at the centre of someone's life. Into the vacuum had stepped what appeared to be the most entertaining, supportive friend I'd ever had, and I didn't mind if she was a bit over the top.

Jack was calling me every few weeks, telling me his woes and hopes. He was using drugs again, and his girlfriend was getting violent. He was working with autistic kids, who were also violent. One day, he had some other news . . .

'Hi, Lins, Jack here. Guess what? I'm having a baby. Well, Matoko is.'

'When?'

'In five months.'

'Did you plan this?'

'Yeah, we did. Sort of . . . it's not that convenient because Matoko's not finished her degree yet . . . but she's going to carry on after she has it.'

'She's going to look after a baby and study full time?'

'Well, Linda,' he said sententiously, 'people do.'

'Very tired people. Why on earth did you want to have a baby now?'

'Well, I thought I might as well do it before I killed myself. You know?'

'No.'

'And, yeah, get this! Her husband's in the picture again. He's decided he wants her back, and he's been writing all these, like, crazed notes. He said he kept waking up in ditches and by roads not knowing how he got there, and he'd been taken in by the police and prescribed medication for psychotic behaviour, but he hadn't taken it coz he couldn't afford the prescription.'

'I see.'

'Yeah, so things might liven up around here a bit.'

I was surprised by how upset I was about the baby. I didn't want one right then and there, but he hadn't wanted one with me and somehow this stranger had convinced him to shackle himself to her for life. It was time to start divorce proceedings and find a new man. I posted a new online ad.

That was when Crazy decided she was sick of affairs and wanted a boyfriend after all. As Duckbill Pete had found to his dismay, she was oddly prudish for a fetish model; within her, I began to see a constant struggle between opposing forces. Her effervescence was fuelled by anxiety, for which she was medicated, and a tenuous sense of her own reality, for which she sought out mirrors, both glass and human. Beneath the glamorous top-coat, she experienced herself as a blank space, but a partner, constantly prevailed upon for reassurance, reflected a solid image she could hold on to. Her relationship pattern was much like her employment and friendships, in which brief ecstatic periods ended with her being 'betrayed'. It never occurred to me that I'd be next in line for the sudden about-turn and character assassination: I was too busy being charmed and fascinated.

She tried her luck at the next Cotton Candy show, which took place in a warehouse exited via a giant slide. The event was organized by the tireless Rob Sparks, a polite gentleman sporting foot-long beard twists with internal structural wiring, and acid-yellow contact lenses. He'd engaged a troupe of dancing clowns to accompany our set, which was dandy until three of them climbed on to the same rope, and a ceiling support threatened to collapse.

As the show unravelled in disarray, Crazy ran up. 'YOU GUYS ARE THE BEST! LINDY-LOO, DO YOU KNOW WHO THAT GUY IS?' She pointed across the room, but I couldn't say, with all the clowns running around, so she went over and tapped his arm anyway. I spotted Johnny Depp, or someone who looked just like him, wearing army surplus, and absently began to follow his beautiful face around the building. While Crazy harangued her victim in the corner, I tracked Johnny into the basement, which was alive with semi-naked people writhing and playing with fire. We were just making our second figure-of-eight when suddenly, from nowhere, Crazy leaped out and grabbed my arm.

'I WAS GREAT! I JUST SAID, "AND WHO ARE YOU?" AND HE SAID, "I'M RHETT," AND I SAID, "WELL, I'M CRAZY! ARE YOU SINGLE?" AND HE SAID, "YES," AND I SAID, "YOU NEEDN'T BE. LET'S TALK."'

'And?'

'NO GOOD! HE WAS SO AMAZED I WAS TALKING TO HIM, BUT HE JUST WASN'T INTELLIGENT ENOUGH, YOU KNOW?'

'That's a shame.'

'I GAVE HIM MY COCKTAIL, AND SAID, "HOLD THIS!" I GUESS HE'S STILL WAITING.'

We looked around for an exit that wasn't a slide.

I got a few responses to my ad. The pick of the blighted crop was Geoff, a tall, blond, blue-eyed, computer-programming, piano-playing painter. Just like Sven. We arranged to meet in a bar on Haight Street, and I arrived a little late, waited twenty minutes and headed home again, fuming.

A cyclist sped over. 'Are you Linda?'

If only I'd had the presence of mind to say, 'No.' This was Geoff, who guided me to the cheapest, most depressing diner in the neighbourhood, where he told me how great he was, while mimicking my accent. He was wearing dirty painting overalls and his lips were so thin they looked like they'd been drawn in red biro. We split the tiny bill. 'So, what happens now?' he said.

'I go home,' I said, and stuck out my hand. 'It was nice meeting you, Geoff.' In order to get my hand back again, I agreed to 'make music' at his place on Wednesday. By the time I got home, he'd already sent me an ardent email, and I wrote straight back, saying that I wasn't going to 'make music' with him, after all. He didn't take it well – in fact, he replied:

Dear Linda

I was expecting you'd say something like that. It seems that my greatest talent lies in putting people off. I have been getting a lot of rejections lately. I wondered if you could tell me what's wrong with me? Please help; I won't take offence.

Dear Geoff

These on-line dates can be soul-destroying, but remember that when someone rejects you, it only tells you about them and their tastes; seeing as you ask, I think it's a good idea to wait in the building, and it's not a good idea to wear your painting overalls or mimic your date's accent.

Dear Linda

Yes. My soul is nearly destroyed, to be honest. I have been stood up so often that it's excruciating to wait more than ten minutes. I just cycled around the block for half an hour, hoping to see you. And the last date I went on, I was really over-dressed, and I didn't want to do it again. But when I saw your outfit, I knew I'd got it wrong again. I suppose if you hate silly accents you'd hate me. I'm going to give up on Internet dating.

But he taught me a valuable lesson: when baking a cake, a banana's a good substitute for an egg.[18]

*

18 As I am allergic to eggs, I take a keen interest in vegan baking techniques.

Crazy had moved on since the slide party.

'I THINK I'VE FOUND HIM, LINDY-LOO! HE'S CALLED DAN! I MET HIM AT THAT PARTY LAST NIGHT, AND I SAID, "CAN I HAVE YOUR NUMBER?" HE SAID, "WELL, YOU CERTAINLY HAVE A LOT TO SAY FOR YOURSELF, DON'T YOU?" WHAT DO YOU THINK THAT MEANS?'

'Well, you're interesting.'

'HE'S SO GREAT. I GOOGLED HIM AND HE'S WRITTEN ALL THESE ADVENTURE STORIES AND I'VE READ THEM ALL ONLINE . . . OH, DO YOU THINK HE LIKES ME?'

But, come Saturday, she was curled up on the sofa. 'Why isn't he calling back, Lins? I told him to call me this weekend. Maybe I should call him up again and tell him I'm not going to chase him . . .'

I was starting to see that 'crazy' didn't just mean wacky. 'Probably. I hope so. But you're wonderful. He's not your only chance.'

She whipped out a headshot she'd printed out from his website. 'Isn't he lovely?'

'Is that a real moustache?'

'He's going to call, isn't he?'

'I hope so, but if not, please don't think it's the end of the—'

'He *has* to call!'

Three days later, she gave up waiting. Her voice, searing at the best of times, echoed through the flat: 'HI, DAN, IT'S ME, CRAZY! I'M CALLING TO SEE WHEN YOU'RE FREE. WE CAN GO OUT ANY TIME, NO PRESSURE. WHAT ARE YOU DOING TOMORROW? . . . WELL, HOW ABOUT SATURDAY? . . . COME ON, YOU CAN SEE YOUR FRIENDS ANY NIGHT — COME OUT WITH ME INSTEAD. I WAS THINKING WE'D CHECK OUT THIS BAR, AND THEN . . .'

She steamrolled her way to a date, but returned in tears. 'He said he's got a broken heart and he's not ready for another relationship! It's so frustrating because we are so perfect for one another. I tried to kiss him and he stood up straight so I couldn't reach. I wanted to die!' She took the next two days off work, claiming 'mental health' days.

Next, she reconsidered her old friend James. Though good-looking and creative, his promiscuity and wild antics had always put her off. 'But what if he's the one, Lins, and I've just overlooked it? What if I made a mistake?' She invited him to our housewarming party where, at midnight, she discovered him sitting on the loo, exposing himself to a small, but enthusiastic crowd. Next, she found him in her bed, taking naked self-portraits. She shooed him off again, but instead of getting dressed, he instigated a highly sexual wrestling bout with his best friend. The pair of them rolled around our bedroom floors, crashing into things and knocking over my bookshelf. 'Maybe it was just a bad night,' she said, and tailed him to a party the next week, where he performed a naked lap-dance for the hostess, who told Crazy his ex-girlfriend had him under a restraining order. 'So I guess he's not really marriage material after all, Lins. Oh, well . . .'

Meanwhile I made a date with a squirrelly man. His ad said he liked tall, elfin women, so I knew he'd like everything about me, except maybe my personality, and I was right about that. Half an hour in he asked me how many people I'd slept with and was horrified by my answer. I was horrified I'd told him. Not only did he make me feel inadequate and prudish, his nervous energy made him sound like a radio ad, his manner was effeminate and he kept mentioning how tall he was. When he said he'd like to see me again, I said yes. Two reasons:

1. A distraction from thinking about Sven so I didn't think about Jack, akin to boring a hole in my skull to relieve a migraine.
2. I felt I needed dating experience of any kind.

Squirrel Man had a neurosis about attracting neurotic women. 'I can't help it. Nutty women are drawn to me. It's a nightmare.' Though I kept quiet about therapy, depression and happy pills, he was sure I had an eating disorder – I was thin, I dressed funny and I'd just had my wisdom teeth out. After three days in bed, existing on a diet of codeine and soup, I agreed to a dinner invitation, and struggled through a potato curry using only my soft palate and tongue. Half-way through, I went to the loo, and he called it a bulimia break. As it happened, I did want to throw up. My jaw ached, I felt sick from too much codeine, there was a cold sore on my lip and a big red lump where I'd smacked my head on a shelf.

'We don't exactly hit it off, do we?' he sniped.

'So why,' I asked, 'do you keep suggesting we meet up again?'

'I don't know. There's something kind of compelling about our interaction, you know?'

'Not really.'

'I mean,' he whined, 'where's the rapport?'

For some reason, I felt responsible, so I took him home and shoved him on to the bed for a test hug – what with the cold sore and the stitches in my gums, I felt safe, but he went for it anyway, rolling his lizard-like tongue over my teeth. 'Have you lost something?' I asked.

'Huh?'

He carried on, saying awful things like 'Yum!' and slobbering around the outside of my mouth. This was going to give me a rash. I broke off and asked where his tongue had got to. 'Well, where are your lips?' he countered.

'On my face.'

'Do you want more *tongue*? Is that what you're saying, Linda?'

I felt something stringy at the back of my mouth and ran to the bathroom. My stitches had just come out, and what with the codeine and the beer, I started giggling. He gave me a stern look. 'Not sexy,' he said, then put his hands in my knickers and started fiddling around. This was as pleasant as a vibrator but, then, vibrators don't make demands.

'I have a front too!' he reminded me.

Never mind his 'front': his back felt like it was covered in giant moles, and when he inexplicably took his top off, this mystery moonscape was revealed to be a raging mass of acne cysts. Didn't he know? Should I tell him? He went home when I started peeling feathers out of the pillow and throwing them at him. He'd told me he was allergic.

Who did I have to choose from? I reviewed my suitors over the past few months:

1. short lesbian who came up to me at a concert and handed me a beer
2. squirrelly guy
3. drunk guy who called me Julie Andrews and wouldn't let go of my hand
4. can't remember but counted it yesterday
5. Geoff
6. short girl with pom-poms all over her head, backstage at a fashion show, who expressed her love when I was dressed as a peacock
7. short photographer in a pork-pie hat
8. short teenager in a costume shop

I was about to despair when I saw I'd received another reply to my ad. Hope springing anew, I clicked the link and saw a picture of a massive black man in tiny swimming trunks and sunglasses. He looked good.

How do I . . .
- Ask your name . . . without emphasizing we are strangers to one another

- Express genuine interest in who you are . . . without appearing out of touch with modern dating
- Impress you with creative writing . . . without leaving the impression of a form letter
- Tell you about myself . . . without the perception of arrogance
- How do I paint a picture to make you smile?

Let me begin with a story. A woman steps into an elevator with a tall well-groomed gentleman. He smiles, she smiles in return . . . shyly at first, then she finds herself lingering on his gentle eyes, his full lips, broad shoulders . . . She pauses for a moment, then bids him a good morning. He smiles and nods in response. He knows little of her, yet he is captivated. He desires nothing less than to ignite her imagination. Leaning closer, he whispers . . . 'My Lady . . . to the east, Borneo . . . to the west, Kuala Lumpur . . . to the south, Jakarta . . . to the north, Saigon. Where are we . . . ?'

He is thirty, attractive and well educated . . . all the basic prerequisites she desires. She is very curious about this gentleman, despite her mother's warnings not to talk to strangers. He is conversant in three languages and well traveled – at last count, twenty countries over the past two years. His purpose in traveling is cultural immersion, not cultural voyeurism . . . i.e., to dine with the locals, to catch local transportation . . . The elevator reaches its destination. As he prepares to step out, he asks . . . 'Would you join me on a sail?' (Destination unknown.) He steps off the elevator . . . his arm softly but intentionally brushes yours. He smiles again, as your sweet scent lingers in his senses . . .

I deleted my profile.

Crazy decided she was going to find me a boyfriend. She dyed my hair pink, popped me into the matching leather dress she'd made for me (with matching gauntlets), and took me to the fetish clown ball. Some girls in body-bags were being whipped in one corner, and a 'naughty nurse' was giving out condoms, though nobody was going to have sex. A middle-aged lady wearing bits of string tried to recruit me for her swingers parties. I hid in the loo for about ten minutes, then forced myself to get back out and sit on a sofa. I started crying when a fat magician told me he had a crush on me, and then Crazy landed on top of me.

'LINDY-LOO! I'VE FOUND YOU A BOYFRIEND! HE'S TALL AND REALLY CUTE. HE'S THIRTY AND HE'S SINGLE AND THE LAST BOOK HE READ WAS BY BUCKMINSTER FULLER.'

'I'm not—'

'COME ON, GET UP. HE'S IN THE NEXT ROOM. THE ONLY PERSON HE KNOWS IS THAT NURSE AND SHE'S BUSY.'

'I haven't—'

'AREN'T YOU PROUD OF ME? I SAID, "HI, I'M CRAZY, WHO ARE YOU? ARE YOU SINGLE? ARE YOU SMART? WHAT ARE YOUR INTELLECTUAL GOALS?"'

'I don't—'

'HE'S NOT GOOD ENOUGH FOR YOU, LINDY-LOO, BUT NO ONE IS: YOU'RE THE BEST. SO I SAID, 'YOU SHOULD DATE MY WIFE! I'LL GO GET HER.' I DID GREAT!'

'I'm not feeling very perky . . .'

'Come on . . .'

'And I'm dressed like a clown, for fuck's sake.'

'Take your nose off. There. And I'll rub off the cold sores. Hold on, I'll get a tissue.'

'Thanks.'

'Come on!'

She skipped off into the next room, then popped her head back round the door. 'AND HE MENTIONED AN EX-GIRLFRIEND, SO HE'S DEFINITELY HAD SEX BEFORE!'

Not a virgin? Maybe there was something in this. I followed in her wake and, sure enough, the New Boyfriend soon floated over. He was wearing normal clothes, which was the sexiest thing to wear

215

in this context. I got nervous, ran off to find alcohol, then positioned myself between him and the exit. It worked. As he told me how good he'd been at playing the trombone in high school, Crazy got a pen, exchanged our contact details, and got him to drive us the four blocks home. He showed me a hat he was knitting that said 'Fuck', and then we were out on the pavement, Crazy yelling, 'THANKS FOR THE RIDE! SEE YOU AT THE COTTON CANDY SHOW!'

He took the pink bait and came to the show the following week. Afterwards, Crazy leaped from the shadows. 'THAT WAS SO GREAT – AMAZING, I'M SO, WOW, IT WAS JUST —' She tugged on the New Boyfriend's sleeve. 'DON'T YOU THINK?'

'Um, yeah,' he said.

'HEY, LINDA NEEDS A RIDE HOME.'

He did as he was told and even carried my accordion into the house.

'This way,' I said, steering him towards my curvy little room. 'Actually, there's something I want to show you in there.' When he put the accordion down, I ran up behind him, shoved him on to the bed, and said, 'It's my ceiling!' Who was this man? It hardly mattered to me – he was pretty, and present. For the last four years, he'd been unemployed, so I set him the task of knitting me a fine mohair scarf; he took to this with relish, and decided to spell out my name in pink and white Morse code. His stock response to me was 'I really like you,' or 'I really, really like you.' This sweetened the bitter truth that our conversations rarely strayed beyond his record collection.

If I had a boyfriend, Crazy had to have one too. She scoured the Internet and found one pronto. Simon liked to lie around, writing, sleeping and eating our food in between having sex with Crazy. He had Crohn's disease, a progressive, painful and incurable bowel disorder, which meant he was always on the toilet. Crazy had constant cystitis with all the sex they were so vocally having, which

216

meant she was constantly in the bath. He joined her often for a candlelit bath-sex-'n'-massage session, and they never pulled the plug – you had to reach your arm into the lukewarm waters of their after-love.

Having switched her fanatical affections from me to him, she guarded his emaciated body with the aggressive jealousy of a mother hen. He was always in our house; for a while she rented out her room and moved into the gargantuan attic with him, where they enjoyed rent-free sex for several weeks. My New Boyfriend was around quite a bit, what with the unemployment, but he tended to keep a low profile, staying in bed knitting, or slinking through the house to smoke outside. But in our open-plan home, there was no avoiding Crazy and Simon, lying naked on the porch, nuzzling on the couch, kissing wetly in the kitchen or lounging in the bathtub like a pair of sea-lions. Apparently, after she'd kept him up all night, Simon had to sleep during the day, and was troubled by the sunshine in Crazy's bedroom, so they moved to Sansa's bed after she'd gone to work. After having sex and bowel problems in her bed all day, they would languish and giggle or watch movies once she got home; she wasn't very assertive, and would sit in the kitchen, waiting for them to leave. Crazy started calling in love-sick to work every other day. They never got dressed. What was the point, when they'd be having sex any second? I'd be in the kitchen eating my lunch while Simon pottered around in his robe, making coffee. Then Crazy would skip in, wearing her slip, put her arms round him and coo, in a baby voice, 'And how are *you*?' One enigma remained – the amount of sex they were having was at odds with Simon's dilapidated physical state. Crohn's disease wasn't best treated with Jim Beam, constant sex and sleep deprivation, but Crazy scoffed at my accusation that he wasn't looking after himself.

'That's so unfair, Linda. Haven't you noticed the olive oil?' A giant can of an organic blend glistened on the shelf. 'It was thirty-five dollars – can we split it?'

217

Simon was a nice boy, really, and it wasn't his fault he was ill, but I began to detest the sight of his tired body and hangdog eyes as he hung around the kitchen, eating the last of my bread.

One day, I climbed into the attic to find Crazy swathed in silver fabric. She beamed at me. 'I'm designing my wedding dress!'

I tried to smile.

'I love him, Lindy-loo! He's just like me – he wants to have sex *all the time*!'

'That's great. Anyway, I'm off to bed.'

I dragged Madam back to my room and lay down with her in an arm-lock as the sex noises started up yet again. They went on and on relentlessly. Crazy's high-pitched, regular 'peep' sounded like a truck in reverse, while Simon was a dying horse. Earplugs helped, but made me feel like a prisoner in my own head and, anyway, I could still hear them in the dead of night. I was so desperate I bought Crazy a ball-gag. 'Thanks,' she tittered, 'but I don't think he'll want to wear it.'

'It's for you.'

How the hell did he keep it up? I got my answer when Crazy confided her safe-sex precautions: two condoms plus a squirt of spermicide, and to hell with the allergic reaction. As far as sensitivity went, he might as well have had his scrotum injected with Novocaine. Poor guy, she was fucking him to death. As his skin turned greenish and craters formed below his eyes, Crazy grew stronger and more vivacious, singing at top volume while she was cutting up his special vegetables or making him a health tonic. In bed and out, she was on top, doing all the work. 'I love Simon, Lins. He's so great.'

'Mmm.'

'Isn't he?'

'Mmm.'

'You do like him, don't you?'

'Mm-hmm.'

'I mean really like him?'

'Mmm.'

'You know what he said to me last night? He said, "If I die, will you have my children?" and of course I would, but I thought it was the saddest thing I'd ever heard. Don't you think?'

Psycho Flatmate

Trouble on the home front? There is nothing worse
Than seeing the friend you live with turn into a curse.
Hide out in your bedroom, tiptoe to the loo,
Since they are blind to reason, there is nothing you can do . . .

Some get obsessive and copy your style;
Take lots of photos and build up a file.
Some get possessive and won't leave your side;
They may want your friends dead but you're deified.

Psycho flatmate, why are you so crazy?
Won't you let me live my life in peace?
Your delusions and demands amaze me,
Will your stupid drama never cease?

Some lose their jobs and start shagging all day,
Hang round the house in their cheap lingerie.
Some contract scabies and blame it on you,
Then take you to court just for something to do.

Psycho flatmate, why are you so crazy? (CRAAAYZEE!!!)
Must you turn my life to total shit?
Your delusions and demands amaze me . . .
I'm no longer willing to submit.

Some try to kill themselves every few months,
They like to feel that you noticed for once.
Some wake you up with their hand down your pants,
Then make you move out if you don't want romance.

Psycho flatmate, why are you so crazy?
I am leaving bitter and perplexed.
Your delusions and demands amaze me . . .
I wonder who you'll get to torture next.

13: The NHS Endurance Test

'I'm so tired these days . . . I just can't be bothered to do anything. It's terrible.'

Mum

There was a new message on our answer machine: 'Hello, I'd like to leave a message for Linda. Linda Robertson. Linda, yes. Tell her that it's Mum. Thank you very much. Goodbye.' When I called her, she said, 'Who's that man on your phone, darling?'

'It's just a recorded message, Mum.'

'Is it an actor?'

'No, it's digital.' I tried to give her another telephone number, and she couldn't get it straight; it was weird. 'Mum,' I said, 'I'll tell you another time. Get some sleep, will you?'

'Yes, darling. I've got to get myself organized.'

I told her Heidi was pregnant. 'Well,' she snapped, 'that puts an end to your little project, doesn't it?'

'Why are you pleased about that? Don't you want me to make music?'

'You should be working, not frittering away your time on such things.'

'I'm trying to, but there are other things that matter too, Mum. Don't you care about the rest of my life?'

She burst into tears. 'I CALL THE PHONE CARD COMPANY TO CHECK MY BALANCE BECAUSE THE VOICE RECORDING SOUNDS JUST LIKE YOU! AND YOU THINK I DON'T CARE!'

221

'Mum, I know you care. I know you love me.'

She seemed to calm down. 'Darling, who's that man on the phone? Is he staying with you?'

Mum's conception of reality had rarely converged with mine, but this was getting bizarre. I didn't know what to think so, as usual, I thought about myself.

I called a few days later.

'Clunkingpalsytwofivesevenfivethreenine.'

'Hi, Dad.'

'Who's this?'

'It's Linda.'

'Oh. Hello, Linda.'

'Where have you been?'

'Your mother and I were away in Dorset for a week.'

'Nobody told me! I was really worried.'

Mum had always told me of their plans; the countdown would begin weeks in advance.

'Er,' said Dad, 'have you heard about your mother?'

'No, what about her?'

'There was a bedside cabinet at our hotel, and she kept asking me to take her things out of it, but it was empty, and then she started on at me to give her the key, but it didn't have a lock, and she kept on like this for *five hours*. She didn't stop till four a.m. Then the next night we were at home, and I woke up to find her in the kitchen, pulling all the things out of the cupboards. At five o'clock in the morning! Five o'clock! I said, "This is bloody ridiculous, come on, Davina, get to bed," but she wouldn't, and she started talking about teapots.'

'She collects them . . .'

'Aye, she does have a lot of teapots. So I took her into the hospital and she's still there now. They're giving her *brain scans*!' His tone was aggrieved and baffled, as though he were complaining about outrageously poor customer service.

'When did this happen?' I asked.

'Oh, about a week ago.'

'Dad! Why didn't you call me?'

'I don't know your number. Your mother's in charge of the phone.'

'Dad, it's in the book in front of you, under R for Robertson.'

'I hear you.'

'Do you see it? The green one. It's right in front of you. R for Robertson.'

'I hear you. Now don't call the ward, Linda.'

'OK . . .'

'And for goodness' sake, DO NOT SEND FLOWERS.'

'Why? Are they not allowed?'

'Now, please, Linda, don't. It's a public ward, it's just not suitable. I'll tell you why I don't approve of flowers – and I know this because I assessed the VAT for a florist in Southampton – the mark-up on delivered flowers is six *hundred* per cent. Six *hundred*!'

'Yes, Dad, I know.' How could I not? It was one of his favourite facts.

Mum had been taken into the psychiatric acute-care ward at Southampton General Hospital. They'd since worked out that she was only insane because her liver was fucked, and her brain wasn't getting fed, and had transferred her to the right ward. As usual, Dad was nonplussed. Like a wind-up toy that had come up against a wall, he kept plodding, feet whirring, getting nowhere. Though even he couldn't deny that something was wrong, he steadfastly maintained, in his own private world, that this situation was a bizarre aberration; that if he just kept whirring, the wall would give way. Davina was just being difficult, as usual.

A week later Alice, my Catholic best friend, called. She'd been round to my parents' house, and had been alarmed by what she saw. She said I'd better get home, so I flew to England. Crazy came too, as my personal assistant, and it was well worth the expense. These were the golden, pre-Simon days. By the time we arrived, Mum was

223

installed in the living room. I walked into the dark green carpeted cave to find her propped up in a chair, grey-skinned and semi-conscious; more a ghost than a mum. Unable to cook or shop, she was starving to death under my dad's indigestible regimen. For the first time I could remember, she didn't smile when she first saw me. She muttered, 'How long are you here for?'

'Five days.'

'Is that all Mother gets? She never spends any time with me . . .'

Maybe she had a point, given my low-impact US lifestyle – and it wasn't as if I had to be anywhere else urgently, but I knew that five days was all my battered psyche could stand. Once I'd slept, I gave her a bath to try to warm her up. They had crappy old plumbing, which couldn't adequately fill the tub without a struggle. As I laboured to get the water hot enough, I fumed that Dad hadn't installed a decent system – another small kindness missed. If the roles had been reversed, she would have got him the most luxurious, sudsy trough on the market.

'Oooh, Linda!' she said, as she sank into the warmth and briefly shone. 'That's lovely! It's the first bath I've had in a year!'

She usually sat on a stool in their mouldy 1970s shower while Dad helped her. I squeezed the sponge over her a few times as the bath turned tepid, and blinked at the sight of her poor, skinny bones. How could that shrivelled, used-up body have played hockey, gone abseiling, made babies and cooked me thirty thousand meals? Now she couldn't even get out of the bath. Crazy had to help me lift her.

Mum was falling apart. Sclerosis had been slowly transforming her lungs and heart to gristle so she couldn't climb the stairs more than one step at a time and struggled for breath at night. And she'd turned really mean. At the dinner table, after she'd choked down a few spoonfuls of custard, she turned to Crazy and said, 'You wouldn't think Linda had gone to Cambridge to look at her now, would you? Didn't do a thing with her degree.'

I'd brought my violin, thinking I'd play it to her, but it never came out of its case. 'I can't believe you brought that all this way. I'm very disappointed in you, Linda. How could you be so stupid?'

'Lindy-loo,' said Crazy, 'however bad you said it was, being at your house is worse than I could have imagined. You were so kind and patient with your mom – the way you spoke to her, I couldn't believe it.'

Dad had become a cipher for all his wife's woes, and she could only express her love for me in terms of fear. She didn't even respond to music any more. I decided to arrange home care and meals for her through the borough council as Dad would not – could not – cope, and made the arrangements when he took her to her check-up at the hospital. To my surprise, he came back alone and dumb-founded. Instead of ticking a piece of paper and sending them home, the doctor had dispatched Mum to the emergency ward.

A day later, they decanted her into the liver ward. We could visit, but no one could tell us what was wrong. Delirious, she pointed to a nurse. 'That one – that's her, Linda! She's trying to make me sick, but I'm not going to let her trick me, ha ha, lady!'

'I'm sure the nurses aren't trying to hurt you, Mum.'

'She is! She's a bitch!'

The evil nurse asked Dad a series of questions about his wife's health. 'What's her appetite been like?'

'Oh,' he said mildly, 'quite good.'

I took her aside and gave her the facts.

Another day, I offered my mother a cup of tea. She was livid. 'No! I can't take that milk!'

'We'll get you skimmed.'

'No! They don't have it. It's all that full fat, which makes me sick but nobody cares, so I can't have tea.'

Crazy piped up, 'I'm sure there must be some somewhere, Mrs Robertson. I'll ask.'

'No! Don't ask. You're not allowed to ask.'

Crazy went anyway, Mum calling in her wake, 'Don't go! There isn't any! Stop her, Alec, stop her.'

She returned shortly, holding a carton aloft. 'Look! They have skimmed milk at the shop, Mrs Robertson.'

Mum wasn't pleased. 'No, they don't.'

I took the milk from Crazy. 'Yes, they do, Mum, look – here it is. So we can get you some tea now.'

'Too late,' she growled. 'The tea lady's gone.'

A couple of hours later we left Mum in the ward, still complaining bitterly about the nurses. As we waved goodbye, she shouted, 'Your father wants me to die!!'

I knew he didn't. He was trying to pretend that Mum only had a cold. I saw, now, that a strange kind of love persisted beyond the mutual disdain. It hadn't crossed my mind that my visit might be good for Dad until later that night when, for the first time in my memory, he gave me an awkward half-hug.

I returned to San Francisco, but a month later I found myself back in Britain. The next day, we visited Mum. Seeing Dad, she snarled the usual 'You again!' To me, she said, 'Oh, Linda, I wish you weren't wearing those socks.'

They were my favourites. I pulled them up and poured her some more water.

On our arrival each day we'd be met with a litany of complaints. 'He didn't bring my orange towel. Your father's a dreadful man! I *need* that towel.'

'Davina, for goodness' sake, you've plenty towels here.'

'I'm not allowed to use them!'

'You are allowed to use them, Mum. Look, I'll get you one.'

She looked up in panic. 'Don't ask her! That's the nurse who wants to kill me!'

Dad sounded weary. 'She doesn't want to kill you, Davina. Now, calm down.'

'What would you know? You put me in here! You want me dead! Where's my dressing-gown?'

She had two. Dad took home a stained one after each visit and brought it back clean the next day. I was flabbergasted. 'Dad,' I said, 'I didn't know you knew how to work the washing-machine.'

He nodded. 'I just attend to everything in the usual efficient manner.'

During each horrendous two-hour visit, Mum made lists of items she wanted us to bring next time, some clear, others mysterious. Her lifelong obsessions with household and transport logistics had taken the controls, generating endless fool's errands for those around her. It was a peculiar fairy-tale, and we strove each day to prove our love by producing the closest approximation to the requested item.

'Where's the green jar? I need the green jar, for Christ's sake! Not that one!'

'What green jar?'

'The green jar, I need it. The doctor said.'

'Where is the green jar, Mum?'

'In the garage. No, in the shed. It's er, er . . . Who said it?'

There had never been a green jar. The only way out of the loop was to change the subject.

I was worried that Mum would die by accident in that place. Since I'd been gone, Dad had designated himself 'feeder', a useless role as she wouldn't eat, but a hospital identity to hold on to. He'd arrive at one p.m. and sit there for an hour, holding a forkful of indigestible tough meat and rubbery vegetables to her clamped lips. 'Come on, Bug, eat. Davina, you've got to eat something.' She'd beat him off with a claw and he'd jab back with another forkful. In the past couple of months, she'd gone down to seven stone (her healthy weight was nine and a half), and as the staff busied themselves conducting endless tests, this seemed to go unnoticed. When I asked, the nutritionist agreed to give her puréed food, but getting her to eat semi-liquid sludge wasn't easy.

The temperature was another worry. She always looked like she'd come out of cold storage – the hospital was nowhere near warm enough for her – and her swollen hands felt like slabs of sausagemeat, fresh from the fridge.

'Are you cold, Mum?' I asked.

'Yes.'

'I'll get you some more blankets. Hold on.'

'No! You're not allowed to use them! She'll be angry!'

I got the blankets anyway, and told a nurse that my mum had to be kept very warm. However, those harried ladies didn't have time to keep people comfortable – it was all they could do to keep anyone alive. No one was ever available to tell me what was going on, and the doctor was eternally 'due in fifteen minutes'. I was forced to get my information filtered through Dad, which was like listening to the radio underwater.

One day I took over the feeding. Instead of eating, she spoke to me: 'Why are you going to Spain, Linda? I don't want you to go.'

'I'm not going to Spain, Mum.'

'Who are you going to go with? Who'll look after you? Flora? I don't trust Flora.'

'Mum, I'm not going to Spain. I'm going to London to see my friends.'

'Can't trust that girl.'

'Mum, I don't think you've even met Flora.'

'Are you not going to Spain?'

'No, I'm going to London, and I'll be fine. How about some soup?'

She thrust it aside. 'It's celery soup. I hate celery!'

'OK. Let's try this, um, stew.'

She licked a few bits off the end of a spoon and spat it out. 'It's disgusting! I can't eat that! It's got celery in it!'

'How about some potato, then?'

'Celery!'

'OK, let's try some of that mousse. Looks like strawberry, that'll be nice.'

She spat it out. 'Celery!'

'Mum, there's no celery in the mousse.'

She gazed at me like a trusting child, and whispered, 'How do you know?'

'Because I asked the chefs. They promised me.'

With ten minutes' intense coaxing, I got her to finish it.

Calcium deposits had made her nails unpleasantly thick; she looked like a long-clawed bird, staring at the other patients and cursing them under her breath between trips to the loo.

'I need the toilet, Linda.'

'OK, Mum, let's go.'

'I'm not allowed.'

Dad sighed. He always tried to reason with her, as though she could snap out of it and be sensible. 'You're allowed to go to the toilet, Bug, for Chrissake.'

'*No*, I'm *not*! I have to go to the one downstairs.'

'There's one up here, Mum, just over there.'

She clung to my shoulder, howling with pain. When it reached its worst, she suddenly remembered my name. 'Oh, Linda!' she whimpered. 'I want to die. I just want to die . . .'

As she had never said it before, I knew she meant it. I didn't reassure her, or say, 'No, you don't.' What was the point? She was stranded on a lonely island of paranoia, amid the cold neutrality of NHS hospitality, and there was nowhere left to go. It's a sad thing to wish your mother dead.

When we arrived at the ward a few days later, Mum had disappeared. I asked a nurse, who said breezily, 'Mrs Robertson? She's having a feeding tube inserted into her stomach. Should be back in ten minutes.'

That was news. Dad and I hung around, forced to listen to the catarrh-choked wheezing of the old lady in the bed opposite Mum's, a sound so theatrically morbid that we started to giggle. We decided to escape the death rattle and go to the cafeteria. As we strolled off, a bed rolled slowly past, on it a shrivelled, bloodless creature, shrouded in institutional linen.

Dad did a double-take. 'Christ, Linda,' he stammered, 'it's your mother!'

I peered down and, yes, he was right. I recognized her ear. I'd never realized before that I even knew what her ears looked like.

As we watched the bed drift away, nurses descended and plugged Mum efficiently back into the ward, and there she lay, criss-crossed with tiny plastic tubes, returned to personhood by the nameplate on her bed. The surgeon had abandoned the stomach-tube idea as she'd proved too fragile. We sat with her for another couple of hours, but she didn't wake up, and we were spared an afternoon's paranoid ravings, which always got worse when we prepared to leave. They were full of fear: 'What's going to happen to me when they put me out at night? They put you out, yes, once a week, they put you out all night! How am I going to cope?'

'They won't put you out anywhere, Mum, I promise. Would I let anybody hurt you?'

'You don't know. They think I'm a loony, but you'll see. It's the Man – he makes a fortune on this place.'

In a gentle but exasperated voice, Dad asked, 'What man, Davina?'

'The Man who owns the hospital.'

'Davina, the hospital's owned by the government.'

'The Man owns the hospital and he's going to sue me for wetting the bed. And they won't let me sleep. I'll be in trouble if I go to sleep.'

I tried to reassure her. 'You can go to sleep, Mum. It's fine.'

'Your father's going to go crazy when he gets the bill.'

'There won't be a bill, Mum, I promise.'

'Please just ask him not to argue with them.'

230

'OK.' I turned to Dad. 'You won't argue when you get the bill, will you, Dad?'

'Ach!' he said, addressing her directly. 'I'll no argue, Bug.'

On my last day, we visited as usual. 'Mum,' I said, 'I'm going to go now. I'm going back to San Francisco tomorrow, but I'll come and see you soon.' I bent down and kissed her. 'Goodbye.'

At once, as if a switch had been flicked back on, she looked me straight in the eye. 'No! I don't want it to be *goodbye*!'

'OK, then,' I said, trying to sound like I was humouring her, 'I'll see you soon.'

'I hate being alone!'

'You'll not be alone, Mum,' I lied. 'There are all the people here, and Dad will come and see you tomorrow, and I'll be back soon.'

Her greying eyes stared in terror; I no longer recognized who or what lay behind them. She was so frail and helpless, an irreplaceable soul in an anonymous gown, adrift in a crisp white sea of institutional linen.

'I love you, Mum.'

'I love you too,' she breathed.

''Bye, Bug,' said Dad, from the end of the bed. 'I'll see you tomorrow.'

'Ach, bugger off.'

'All right, I'll bugger off, then.'

Her angry voice followed us out of the ward: 'Do you have to go?'

Dad turned. 'Ach, Davina! We've been here two hours already. I'll be here to see you tomorrow.'

'Can you not stay here with me?'

If she'd seemed at all pleased by my presence, I might have found the strength to stay. Instead I let out a little 'Goodbye' and walked quickly away.

*

Once I was back in the States, Dad kept me abreast of events at the hospital. We spoke every few days. 'Your mother keeps saying she's on the wrong ship. She tried to throw her food out of the window last night.'

'You're very patient with her, Dad.'

He didn't know how to handle praise. 'Aye . . . aye. Nothing else to report.' He was brief to the point of absurdity on the phone, as though the mouthpiece was on fire. So when he called me one day at the end of the summer, about a month later, I knew something was up. It was the first phone call he'd made to me in his life.

'Hello, Linda, it's Dad. I'm sorry to say your mother died about an hour ago. Internal haemorrhaging. She bled to death. They said it's a standard way to go with her condition.'

'Oh, Dad, I'm sorry you're having to go through this.' *What am I saying?*

'I can hardly believe it, Linda – I thought she'd outlive me.'

'You did?'

'Aye.' He spoke in a newscaster's monotone. 'They offered me the option of keeping her heart going artificially, but they said she'd only last a couple of weeks, so I took the rather cruel decision of saying no.'

'You made the right one, Dad.'

'Anyway, we'll be having a cremation service.'

'When'll that be?'

'Friday, but – no, don't come over for it, Linda.'

'Dad, are you suggesting I miss my mother's funeral?'

'Ach, it's an awful expense, coming all that way again.'

I tried a different tack. 'You know, I'd like to come over and stay for a bit. I could cook for you, help you organize things.'

'Oh, aye, that would be very nice.'

'OK, well, you look after yourself, Dad. I'll call you soon to tell you when I'm coming.' I sank to the floor, a shuddering pile of orange and yellow stripes.

When the ground stopped moving, I picked myself up and started looking for a plane ticket.

A couple of days later, I was in England with Dad. I cooked him food with meat and potatoes and we went to Winchester Cathedral, where we each surreptitiously lit a candle. I'd always wanted to do that as a child, but Mum and Dad had said it was a load of nonsense. I looked at the written requests.

- Dear God, please look after my gran's cat who is ill. She is eighty-nine and will be very sad.
- Heavenly Father, help my friend Ramona with her dissertation.

That next night, we played snooker, and he removed any balls that stood in my way, or else put things back so I could take another shot. 'Come on, lassie, you can do better than that!' We hadn't had such a good time since he'd taught me to fly a kite in 1978.

The next morning, the vicar came round, and I filled her in on stuff Dad didn't know, like Mum's skills, interests, accomplishments and passions, and whether or not she believed in God. After that, Dad stank the place out with a boil-in-the-bag kipper, so I suggested a walk.

As we circled the lake, he started talking about death. His parents, his son, his brother, half of his colleagues and now his wife were all dead. He was alive, and there was absolutely *nothing* wrong with him. 'I shook a man's hand at the bowling club the other day, and he recoiled in pain. He had arthritis in his hand, and he said to me, "When you get to my age, Alec, you'll know what it's about." Turns out he's sixty-seven.' Dad was seventy-two at the time. His diet consisted mainly of fish and beer, like that of a sociable penguin. If greenery landed on his plate, he viewed it as decoration, as likely to be eaten as the tablecloth. In this way, he took in a thousand calories a day, and kept on walking, walking, walking.

The following day, he showed me his collection of pre-electric sewing-machines, which he kept in the shed. 'Got this one for a pound at the car-boot sale. All it needed was a wee skoosh of oil, and it works perfectly!'

'Wow! It's beautiful.'

He wanted me to take one of these leaden treasures back on the plane, but I refused, and he told me he'd once filled one of Mum's old perfume bottles with engine oil for the machines, and she'd found it in the bedroom. 'She used to dab it behind her ears.'

'Dad! Did you not tell her?'

'No, no, she seemed perfectly happy.'

We drove to the undertaker's, where I cancelled Dad's pastel flowers and ordered three times as many in orange, red and yellow. After a brief struggle, he gave in, saying, 'Well, it's a once-in-a-lifetime thing.' Birthdays and anniversaries always come back to haunt you, but you're safe with a corpse.

The undertaker explained that ours was decomposing so fast he'd have to nail down the lid in a few hours' time. 'I'm so sorry, it just happens like this sometimes. It's most unfortunate. Once again, I do apologize.' As he backed off, we went into the little 'chapel'. There was the familiar, prosaic symbol of the incomprehensible. With its golden handles and glossy surface, the box made her death more real than its contents could. As I sobbed quietly, Dad chortled with embarrassment, and started up like a BBC commentator at a royal wedding, delivering respectful platitudes in soft tones – anything to stop himself crying.

'Well . . . you'll never see a sadder sight than that.'

'Mmp.'

'So, that's your mother.' He rubbed his index finger down her nose. 'I've done that so many times . . .'

Yes, and she hated it. ' . . .'

'Feel how cold she is, Linda – incredibly cold!'

' . . .'

234

'Goodbye,' he said, stroking her hair with one finger. 'You're a good girl . . .'

' . . .'

'Good girl . . .'

' . . .'

'Agh, you'll never see a sadder sight than that . . .'

'Mmp.'

'. . . You'll never see a sadder sight than that . . .'

' . . .'

'Feel how cold she is, terribly cold!'

I felt what had been her face. It was as cold as her hands always were.

'Terribly cold!' said Dad, as though surprised.

' . . .'

'You're a good girl, Davina. A good girl.'

' . . .'

'Kiss your mother, Linda.'

We left her in the chapel and they nailed down the lid. Nobody else got to see her.

Twenty minutes later we were at home, sitting in the sun in the garden, swinging on the swing-seat with a couple of beers. Dad burped and put his can on the grass. 'I can hardly believe she's gone, Linda. I just can't believe it. I thought she was coming home,' he said. 'I've been keeping all her houseplants alive. I guess I'll throw them out now. They're an awful scutter.' Above our heads, a million maple leaves swished past each other.

He sighed with them. 'Old Bug. I wasn't sympathetic enough, I suppose.'

The next day, grey skies hung overhead as our garden filled up with friends and relatives. They included Mum's six half-brothers and sisters and most of their kids, and it was surprisingly comforting to see them, even though we had never spoken about anything except biscuits and the weather. The arrival of the hearse, gleaming black and stuffed with brilliant flowers, was the worst moment, and two of the aunts materialized unbidden, ready to hold me in case I crumpled to the floor. 'The poor cow! She had to die to get flowers off Dad!'

We packed into a fleet of cars and followed the hearse to the crematorium, which looked like a factory. The place was packed. After the first hymn, Dad went to the front and lurched through his speech: 'We were married for forty-three years and I can hardly believe she's gone. I always thought she would outlive me. When I first met Davina, she was extremely fit. In fact, she had just completed an intensive course to be a PE teacher. She was also a fairly accomplished pianist. But, sadly, she died recently.'

After the ceremony, as the mourners filed past the flowers, my uncle Van told me he'd been cast as the lead understudy in the West Riding Gilbert and Sullivan Society's production of *The Mikado*: 'And the guy who was in the lead, he stepped back to admire the set and he fell right off the stage! Broke his leg, so I got the role, and – I'm being totally honest with you now – it really was, truly, the most exciting week in my life. *The* most exciting week in my life, I really truly mean that, Davin— er, Linda. Really wonderful. You know *The Mikado*?'

'No.'

He sang me an excerpt. 'You know, "We are Siamese if you please! We are Siamese if you don't please"!'

'Um. I have to speak to the vicar.'

Dad drove us home slowly. 'The worst day of my life.'

'Your speech was really good, Dad. You did a great job.'

'Yes. I wasn't looking forward to it, I can tell you. Fortunately, I've done public speaking before.'

'When was that?'

'When they introduced VAT in 1973, I had to talk to members of the public to explain it all. People said I was a very clear speaker.'

Interflora

You arrived that day in a big black car
Stuffed with brilliant bouquets.
Happy colour was screaming forth
On the greyest of days.

Standing in the driveway, I thought how sad
That you had to die to get some flowers off Dad.

'I never buy flowers,' he liked to say,
'The mark-up's six hundred per cent!'
But this, he noted duly, was well and truly
A once-in-a-lifetime event.

But his hand in mine still shook,
As the vicar read from the turgid book.

Then Dad made a halting speech
About his healthy bride,
Who lived with him for forty-three years
And then, unfortunately, died.

The sandwiches were excellent at our little wake,
You were done and dusted and everyone ate cake.

When everyone had left, I looked through all the old photographs. I found one of Mum as a ringleted tot sitting in a mass of tulips, then one from ten years back, laughing while Dad snapped her on a Porta Potti. Wiping my eyes for the thousandth time, I opened a suitcase full of letters and postcards she'd sent me over the years. When I'd first gone to college, she'd nearly had a breakdown and had written to me every day – notes, cuttings from the *Daily*

Telegraph and endless postcards. She'd studied history of art to 'keep up' with me, and I'd get little renditions of Klimt and Schiele in my pigeon-hole. At the time, I regarded them as little more exciting than junk mail; a paper manifestation of her loneliness. Now each was a tiny, irreplaceable treasure. Sitting on the floor, I picked one at random and began to read.

> *Dear Linda,*
> *Just your silly mother saying 'hello' to you! I had a spare card so I thought I'd utilize it. Do you like the pink flowers? That's gypsophila; we have some in the garden. Well, the post goes soon, so I'm going to curtail my little missive. Make sure you get your inhaler from the doctor; you must look after your health, my darling.*
> *Love, Mum XXXXXXXXXXXX*

14: Pink Gold

'Remember that your mother loves you and you are
brilliant. *You go for it, my darling.'*

Mum

I'd got a special 'funeral deal' with BA, who bumped me up to business
class when I whipped out the death certificate. Stretched out on my
own bed, with its retractable entertainment-module, and discussing
my choice of white wine with the waiters, I forgot to cry for about four
hours; when I remembered, they ushered me into the first-class loo.

I finally arrived home, dragged my suitcase up the steps and
trudged to the bathroom where, to my dismay, I found Crazy. She was
sitting in the bath, neck-high in bubbles, while Simon sat solicitously
by the tub, holding her hand. 'Lins – I just got fired!' she blubbed.

I can't say I was surprised. In the past month, if she'd made it
out of the front door, she'd been two hours late, with makeup down
her face and a gynaecologist's appointment at three thirty. 'It's totally
unfair!' She splashed. 'My boss said I wasn't focusing on the job!'

Simon sensed that my mind was elsewhere, and asked how the
funeral had been, at which I launched into my tale of woe and
ended up with a plea: 'So I could really do with a bath. Are you two
gonna be long?'

Crazy brought her knees up to her chest and her face hardened.
'I know it sucks to lose your mom, Linda, but you're not the only
one who's having a hard time right now.'

With Mum gone, there was no one between me and the clouds; I was out on my own. Life was going to run out, like milk, and I no longer had time for this crap. 'I know it sucks to lose your job,' I said, 'but you can go and get another, can't you?' *If only*, added my brain, *you could stop fucking your boyfriend for long enough to get to an interview.*

Crazy reared up in her bank of foam. 'EVER SINCE YOUR MOM WENT MAD, YOU'VE BEEN ALL SULLEN AND GLOOMY AND IT MAKES ME FEEL AWFUL! I HATE IT WHEN YOU'RE ANGRY WITH ME!!'

'I'm not angry. I'm sad. And it's not about you. Can't you just let me get on with it?'

'SHE'S YELLING AT ME AGAIN, SIMON!'

'No, I'm not,' I said.

'And you make Simon feel uncomfortable in the apartment. HE DOESN'T FEEL AT HOME!'

'Well, he shouldn't, 'coz he's *not*!'

My cardboard stockade had started to collapse. I held things together during the day, but at night grief crept under the covers and shook me like an icy fever. Woken by the commotion, my New Boyfriend would wrap his arms round me until it passed. We spent the next couple of months in bed, drinking whisky and working our way through his vast collection of kung-fu movies. But for the next year, at least, it was as though I was carrying around a cup of the tepid sugar solution Mum had called tea, full to the brim and overflowing at the slightest jolt. I thought the tears would wear tracks down my cheeks.

I heard that the 14th Annual San Francisco Accordion Festival was coming up. The long-dead Ms San Francisco Accordion Pageant was to be revived. Samuel Squeeze was in charge, and he thought I was in with a chance: 'There's only one other competitor so far. Do you know Kielbasia?' I was up against a transvestite, so I knew it'd be tough, but I was determined to win the plastic crown. I began working on my song.

On the day itself, Cotton Candy played a set just before the pageant started. That meant I had a bevy of supporters on hand, including a few violin students and the supervisors from my new volunteer job at the psychiatric hospital, all of whom enjoyed seeing me look silly. As soon as we'd finished playing, I rushed off to the green room, where I exchanged a humdrum gingham dress for a glossy pink ballgown: ruffles *everywhere*. Then I squeezed into polka-dot high-heels and tottered back to Tom and Matt (the malleting marimba player with the frilly cuffs), in time to hear Samuel Squeeze introducing my rivals.

'And so, please give a warm welcome to contestant number one, Kielbasia from Wontzabiglik!'

On to the stage strutted my biggest rival, to gales of delighted laughter. He had shaved his hands specially, and wore a bouffant wig and comedy glasses, plus a 'glamorous dinner-lady' top, hand-sewn for the occasion, with batwing sleeves. I couldn't beat that.

Heidi squeezed my shoulder. 'Don't worry, Linsikins. It's not your fault – you just can't beat a tranny in this town.'

When the crowd quietened down, Kielbasia struck up a song about his charitable sausage-selling scheme, set up in aid of the poor orphans of Wontzabiglik, back in Poland.

> We're stuffing our skins for the poor little children,
> We're selling our sausages cheap.
> If anyone asks, I'll deliver the goods,
> And push it in nice and deep!

I watched with a grim, professional eye. 'He's not played a single wrong note, Tom, not one.'

He put his arm round me. 'You're prettier, Pumpkin.'

'Only just.'

'And don't forget,' piped up Matt, 'you have a sparkly silver accordion with pink bellows!'

Heidi patted my hand. 'And your song, Lindy-loo – you have a sweet little song.'

'It's not rude, though!' I smacked my hand against my forehead. 'This is supposed to be a family show but, apparently, a tranny making sausage gags is just fine! That's arse-fucking!'

Kielbasia left the stage to tumultuous applause. At last it was my turn. 'Go, go!' Heidi pushed me towards the stage. 'Break a leg!'

'She just might, in those shoes,' observed Matt.

Samuel Squeeze welcomed me to the stage. 'So, tell me, Linda, what is it that you like about the accordion?'

I took a deep breath. 'Well, Sam, I was having boyfriend trouble a few years back and I wanted to find something to squeeze that couldn't get away from me.'

There was an *aah* of sympathy from the audience.

'I see,' nodded Samuel, and it was time for my song. The pressure was overwhelming. What with the future of the band at stake – our shows had been attracting single-digit audiences for some time now – and the audience and the man from the accordion store at the back, and all my students and everyone looking at me, I felt dizzy – but I'd already started playing the introduction and there was no going back.

Ms Accordion 2004

When I was a small girl, I used to dream,
Of cotton-candy clouds and polka-dot ice—

Oh, yes, there was. I'd fucked up the tune. OK, back to the beginning . . .

Ms Accordion 2004

When I was a small girl, I used to dream,
Of cotton-candy clouds and polka-dot ice-cream.
Now I'm a grown-up, I want nothing more
Than to be Ms Accordion 2004!

I'm going to press all the right buttons; I'm going to hit all the right
  notes,
I will do most anything to get a few more votes!
I'm going to fill this town with sparkles; I'm going to pump it full of joy,
Totally oblivious to those whom I annoy.
I'm going to squeeze this city breathless; I'm going to play for all I'm
  worth,
Coz the accordion's the greatest little instrument on earth!

Buzzing with adrenalin as though I'd just walked from a fatal car wreck, I curtsied and left the stage, saying a secret prayer of thanks that I'd survived the ordeal.

'Lindy-loo, you were great!'

'Good job, Pumpkin!'

'Do you think they liked it?' I asked breathlessly.

Heidi nodded. 'Course they did. If you weren't up against a tranny, you'd have won, no doubt.'

A real woman dressed as a hippie got on stage and performed something to do with Janis Joplin – I couldn't work it out. The crowd seemed restless, and Tom was confident things would go well.

'Don't worry, Pumpkin, second place is in the bag.'

'Well, there's one more competitor,' I reminded him. 'I don't know who it is.'

'No one who can touch you.'

Suddenly a huge round of applause erupted, and we looked to the stage to see a curvaceous brunette with big lips, wearing the bottom half of a leather bikini, fishnet stockings, garters and six-inch platforms. The accordion was the only thing between us and her chest. To top it off, a whip and a pair of handcuffs dangled from her wrist. My mouth hung open. 'Oh no,' I breathed.

Heidi shook her head. 'Shit on a goddamn stick! Now you'll be third.'

'Wow,' said Tom. 'I wish she didn't have that damned accordion on.'

Matt wasn't impressed. 'Oh, come on, people, that girl is a moose.'

Samuel Squeeze was in Tom's camp. In fact, he'd gone a bit red in the face. 'Well, Anastasia,' he said, 'that's quite an outfit you, err, have on.'

She smiled. 'Thanks, Sam!'

'May I ask what happened to the top half?'

'My accordion's all I need to keep me warm.'

Matt stubbed out his cigarette. 'For Godsakes, it's just a woman in a goddamn swimsuit.'

'Matt, she's a doll,' whispered Tom.

'Tom, that is not a doll. *That* is a viper.'

Heidi shushed them. 'Come on, let's listen.'

Sam turned to the beauty and asked his first official question: 'So, why do you like the accordion, Anastasia?'

'Because I love a good strong squeeze, Sam.' There were wolf-whistles and cries of 'Take it off!' She flicked her dark locks in response.

'Now can you tell us why you should be Ms Accordion 2004?'

'Because I intend to dominate this city with lashings of accordion music!'

A massive round of applause and more whistles.

'She's so fucking full of herself!' hissed Matt.

She had confidence, all right, and a low, sultry voice; a little off-pitch, but you can't have everything.

I strap you on my body; I do the buckles tight,
And pump your loving music, baby, all through the night.

My head drooped. 'I'm sorry. I tried.'

Heidi gave me a hug. 'That's OK, Lindy-loo. You did your best, and you never know, you might still beat her.'

I nodded. 'Her chord structures were pretty bland.'

'Yeah,' Tom grinned, 'but look at the rest of her structure!' He chortled as Anastasia stalked off the stage. 'Check out those buns!'

'What are you talking about?' scoffed Matt. 'We're gonna beat that bitch!'

Samuel Squeeze stepped forward once again, a solemn cast to his ruddy features. 'OK, ladies and gentlemen,' he crowed, 'it's time for you guys to pick a winner. Um, whoever gets the loudest cheer will be crowned the new Ms San Francisco Accordion, so reach deep into your, um, voice-boxes!'

'Damn it!' I kicked off my stupid shoes. 'Why didn't I do something rude?'

Then Samuel called each contestant back to the stage, and I had to get my shoes back on. As I stood there, teetering between my rivals in a frenzy of pastel tulle, I imagined the caption: 'Pitiful in Pink'. Still, I tried to rearrange my face to look positive. Samuel reprised for the crowd each contestant's talents and special features, and the crowd yelled in response. Hippie Lady did OK, then the transvestite did a bit better, and then Anastasia generated a massive whooping cheer. *Quelle surprise.* With a sigh, I looked up, expecting rain. Then I heard: 'And all the way from England, it's Miss Pink, Linda Robertson from Cotton Candy. What do you think of her?'

To my amazement, the crowd went crazy all over again.

'I can't hear you!' he cried.

'*Yaaaaay!*'

It had come down to a face-off between myself and Anastasia.

245

This was fortunate for me as it hinged upon our improvisational wit, for which a British accent – on the California stage – is a good stand-in.

'And why, Linda from Cotton Candy, should people vote for you?'

'Because I'm going to ask nicely.' I turned to the crowd and did my best Emma Thompson voice. 'Good afternoon, ladies and gentlemen. I should be very grateful if you would consider voting for me.'

Big tits be damned, Anastasia couldn't match that. Neither did she have a dedicated team of middle-aged mental-health workers and their families pitching for her, anxious to have someone with a title at the office. 'And the winner is . . .' Samuel raised my delicate wrist into the air '. . . Ms Linda Robertson!'

I stepped forward as the new Ms San Francisco Accordion 2004 and accepted my plastic crown. My acceptance speech was brief. 'Thank you very much. I'm elated! I'd like to thank my wonderful cohorts here on stage, and my students and supervisors for showing up to laugh at me, and my wonderful bandmates and the man from the accordion shop, who'll maybe give me a discount now. Thank you!'

I rushed over to join the band, clutching a stash of vouchers and a plastic sceptre. Heidi hugged me. 'You did it! I'm so proud of you, Lindy-loo!'

Tom was blown away. 'I can't believe it.'

'I can,' sniffed Matt.

'What do you know? You're gay.'

'Exactly. All the straight men voted for that whore, but how many straight men will you find at an accordion festival?'

'Enough to make all those cat-calls.'

'A high-profile minority, obviously.'

'And there's all the women and the kids,' said Heidi. 'I guess we didn't think of that.'

My long-suffering students came over and congratulated me, and a few extra friends I hadn't known about. As I stood there in my sparkly plastic tiara, clutching a raggled bouquet, I realized I was surrounded by people. These were my friends, and San Francisco was my home. I could probably steer my own way out of the rest of the shit.

I started when I got home. Sven had finally sent a thank-you for his birthday present. He'd been away for a few months, with his computer, and had only just opened my package. He'd told his mum he didn't believe in God and he was 'still dating Carla'. Still?

> Dear Sven
> Madam has a new boyfriend, as do I. He used to be good at the
> trombone and is completely infatuated with me and tells me all about
> it, which makes me smile. Love, Linda XX
> PS I am Ms San Francisco Accordion 2004.

I had no more tolerance for Crazy's antics. I extricated myself from her orbit and moved into a tiny studio with an accordion, a violin and a suitcase, into which the bed fitted like a new toaster in its box. I couldn't even take my cat.

My dad had already bought a ticket to the USA and arrived a week later. Short of sharing a bed, I had nowhere to put him and, to save him the cost of a hotel, secured him a cat-sitting job in a pink palace of an apartment. There, surrounded by pictures of Liberace, he spent two slightly nonplussed weeks with the puffiest, most glamorous of pampered felines, which I plied with gourmet food and epilepsy tablets twice a day.

I cleaned a lot of things out with that move; once the New Boyfriend had helped manhandle my possessions across the city, I took my scarf and jettisoned him. 'Was it the sex?' he asked. I assured him that it was everything else.

Next, I drew on my extensive experience in CV fictionalization and convinced California State University that I was a kind, caring, helping type. They agreed to take me on and pay my fees so that I could get my therapist's job. In my first psychology class, I learned that Crazy met the criteria for diagnoses of Histrionic, Borderline and Narcissistic personality disorders.

Oh, and Jack wrote to me:

Dear Linda
It means more to me than I can easily explain to have you as
a friend, because I still love you more than I could ever love
anybody else. You're the wonderfullest person in the world –
the most lovely, the most precious and the most fun.
Love, Jack XX

We spoke on the phone, and he told me about his continued strife:

1. He'd been spending $100 a week on drugs when his take-home was less than $300.
2. After the baby was born, Matoko had got really angry and had started hitting him, so they had been going to a counsellor for domestic violence resolution.
3. The recurrence of the situation he'd known with me had made him realize that he was a 'grumpy sod' and that a lot of our arguing had been to do with him and his drinking problems.
4. He had been letting the drink get out of hand again and recently fell unconscious in the street and was picked up by the police who started beating him up and arrested him for resisting arrest. His head was hurt so badly he had to have an MRI scan, and represented himself in court.

'That's it, Lins, never again.'
'Mmm.'

'How's the book going? I'd be happy to read it through for you, you know, give you a few editorial pointers. Besides, I'm interested in seeing if you've got everything right about me.'

'Oh, don't worry,' I said. 'I have.'

Acknowledgements:

I'm indebted to many people for the fact of this book. Firstly to my editor, Mitzi Angel, for having the vision to spot a story within a slab of anecdotes, and the patience to help me carve it out. Secondly to my bandmates, flatmates and friends for reading, re-reading, laughing, not laughing, reading the entire thing again, and still being sweet about it. And lastly to my mum and dad, for giving me things to say, and encouraging me to say them.

Can you hear the music?

All of the songs in this book are performed by the author's bands, Cotton Candy and The Trifles. You can find out more at www.cottoncandycabaret.com and www.thetrifles.com, download songs at www.myspace.com/cottoncandycabaret and www.myspace.com/thetrifles or buy CDs at www.cdbaby.com

Index

255

Index of Songs